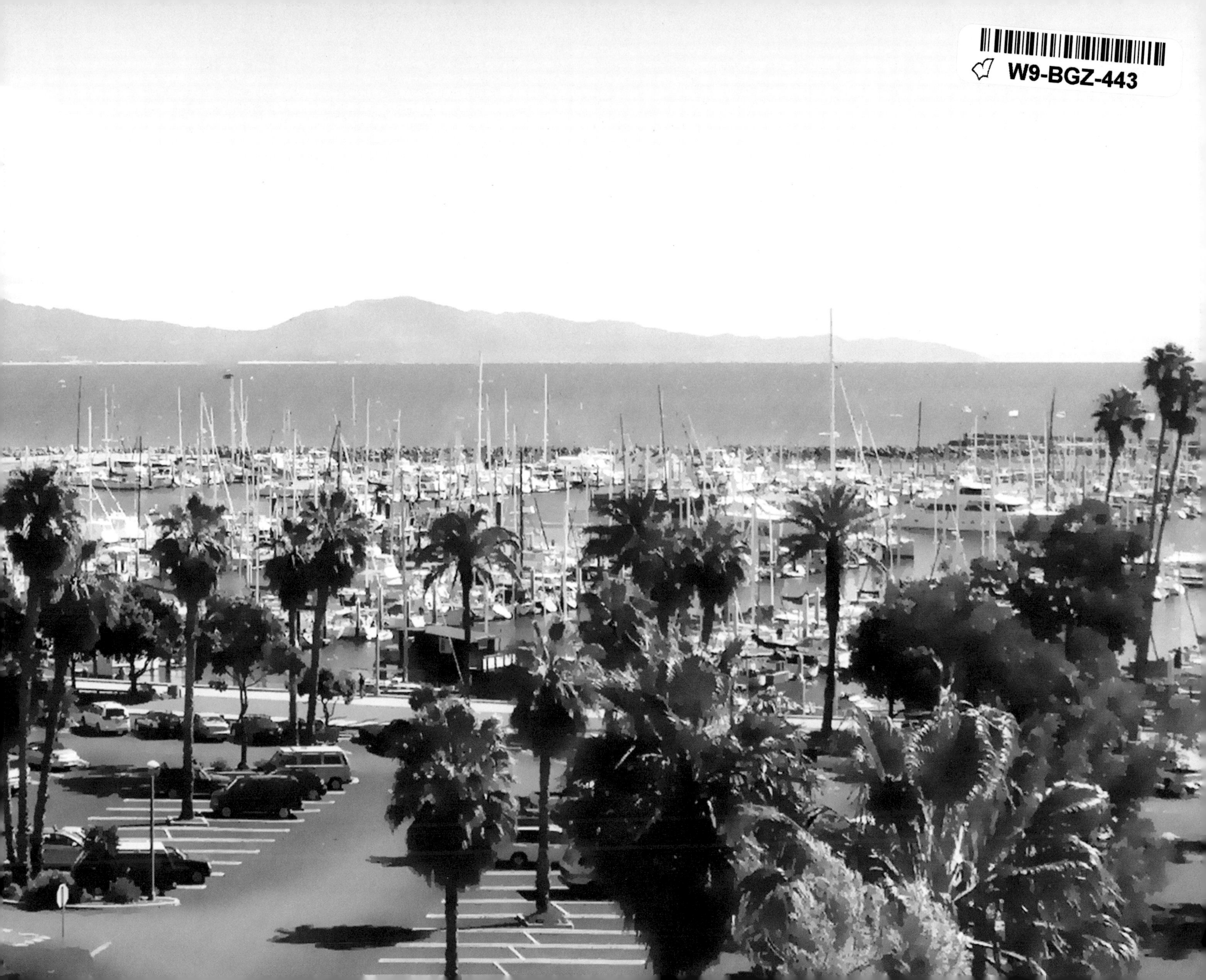

SANTA BARBARA CULINARY ARTS

A Taste of Santa Barbara's Culinary Bounty
Edition II

SANTA BARBARA CULINARY ARTS A Taste of Santa Barbara's Culinary Bounty, Edition II by Tama Takahashi

Books may be purchased by contacting Santa Barbara Culinary Arts, at PO Box 92232, Santa Barbara, CA 93190-2232 or by email at santabarbaraculinaryarts@yahoo.com

Printed by: DeHarts Media Services, San Jose, CA

Design and Editing by: Tama Takahashi
Photography by: Linda Blue

Produced by the nonprofit Santa Barbara Culinary Arts
www.santabarbaraculinaryarts.com
santabarbaraculinaryarts@yahoo.com

ISBN-10:0692519688
ISBN-13:978-0-692-51968-4

Second Edition
Printed in the USA

SANTA BARBARA CULINARY ARTS

A Taste of Santa Barbara's Culinary Bounty
Edition II

Designed and Edited by TAMA TAKAHASHI
Photographed by LINDA BLUE
Produced by the nonprofit Santa Barbara Culinary Arts

Santa Barbara Culinary Arts Board of Directors:

Karyn Yule, Co-President
Cory O'Neill, Co-President
Terry Thomas, Treasurer
Judy Edner, Secretary
Bonnie Crouse, Membership Chair
Gretchen Hewlett, Liaison, Santa Barbara City College
Marilyn Zellet, Board Member
Pam Stowe, Board Member
Tama Takahashi, Cookbook Editor

Mission Statement:

Santa Barbara Culinary Arts is a nonprofit organization dedicated to the inspiration, education and celebration of culinary professionals and individuals who are passionate about the culinary arts.

Highlights of the Santa Barbara Culinary Arts Group:

- Culinary events featuring local chefs and their specialties, as well as cooking demonstrations and instruction
- Learn about new restaurants spotlighted throughout the year
- Networking opportunities at SBCA events while enjoying delicious food, wine and educational programs
- Participation in our fundraising events, such as the sold-out cookbook launch party
- Member support and event attendance enables SBCA to continue our endowment of the Santa Barbara Culinary Arts Scholarship in Honor of Julia Child. This endowment fund provides annual scholarships to the Santa Barbara City College Culinary Arts program.

Membership Benefits:

- Member discounts at SBCA events
- "Members only" events
- Website link to your business and email listing with business bio in members-only data base
- Notices regarding your food-related business emailed to members (now hiring/job needed/equipment for sale/needed, etc.)
- Networking opportunities with local chefs, restaurateurs, food and wine purveyors as well as other professionals and enthusiasts

SANTA BARBARA CULINARY ARTS

P.O. Box 92232
Santa Barbara, CA 93190-2232
www.santabarbaraculinaryarts.com
santabarbaraculinaryarts@yahoo.com

805.895.6750

The Southern Central Coast of California is a feast for the eyes and for the palate. International visitors are charmed by our elegant Spanish Colonial architecture, our shaded lanes splashed with the color of year-round flowers, our broad beaches fronting the glittering Pacific Ocean and our coastal mountain range vistas. We celebrate food and wine with a wide range of events including, but not limited to, Old Spanish Days Fiesta, the Harbor & Seafood Festival, Taste of Solvang, the Santa Barbara Vintners' Festivals, Taste of the Town, the Fermentation Festival, Santa Barbara Food & Wine Weekend, the Santa Barbara Wine Festival and the month-long epicure.SB devoted to sampling our many fine restaurants.

At the meeting point of land and sea, our area borders one of the great fishing grounds of the world. The rich Santa Barbara Channel provides an abundance of sustainable, high-quality seafood including Santa Barbara spot prawns and uni. The land and climate of California makes it an agricultural powerhouse. It is one of only five major regions in the world with a Mediterranean climate where fresh fruits and vegetables can be produced every month of the year. Besides provisioning our kitchens with local organic produce, we are less than 2 hours from the San Joaquin Valley, the world's largest area of Class 1 soil (the highest capability classification) growing an astonishing diversity of produce. We are blessed by nature with both beauty and bounty.

At least two things are needed to support an epicurean culture: fresh, delicious ingredients and money. Our area has both. In the city of Santa Barbara alone, according to the 2013 Santa Barbara South Coast Visitor Industry Economic Impact Model, visitors spend on average $4 million a day, 86% of it dining in restaurants.

The confluence of nature's blessings and a thriving economy has led to robust and delightful dining scene. Underpinning it are the growers, markets, food purveyors and wholesale distributors like The Berry Man, Inc. which supplies local and exotic produce to our fine restaurants and caterers. SBCA would like to express our deep appreciation to The Berry Man Inc. for sponsoring this cookbook as well as supporting many of our fundraising events, such as the ever-popular Mushroom Madness dinner and our cooking demo with three of the best executive chefs in the area representing The Stonehouse at San Ysidro Ranch, The Valley Club of Montecito and Bella Vista the Biltmore at Four Seasons. Santa Barbara Culinary Arts chef demos, cooking classes and dinners are open to the public. Please join in one of our next events and help support our local culinary students through our scholarship endowment: www.meetup.com/santa-Barbara-Culinary-Arts

Acknowledgements

Our region encompasses the vineyards and strawberry fields of Santa Maria, the diverse wine trails of Santa Ynez Valley, Santa Barbara: the elegant jewel of the "American Riviera", charming Ventura and the perfect small town of Ojai. Whether digging into a savory, spicy bowl of posole at the Our Lady of Guadalupe during Fiesta, popping into Opal for a post-theater crab cake, piling your plate with brunch delicacies on the sun-washed patio at the Biltmore Four Seasons or reserving a four-course, wine-paired meal at the John Dunn Gourmet Dining Room at SBCC, culinary delights await. Dig in!

Some say the term "foodie" is passe, but the idea behind a comment I overheard recently over the din of a convivial restaurant holds true: "If you live in Santa Barbara, you are a foodie by definition because Santa Barbara is a foodie town". Great food and wine are part of our lifestyle and some of the best can be found at the potluck dinner before our monthly Santa Barbara Culinary Arts board meeting. Our board members are a dedicated group of culinary professionals with a passion for raising money for good causes. This year our endowment fund, Santa Barbara Culinary Arts Scholarship in Honor of Julia Child, grew by $22,500 -- $15,000 from funds raised through last year's successful, sold out cookbook plus $7,500 provided in matching grant funds by the Santa Barbara City College Foundation. The School of Culinary Arts & Hotel Management is an integral part of sustaining the vibrant culinary scene and we are proud to help support local culinary students in their quest to contribute. We are obliged to the chefs, caterers, restaurants and wineries that contributed to this cookbook, participating in this worthy and tasty endeavor both this year and last.

Many thanks to all the members of the Board of Santa Barbara Culinary Arts for their support of this project and their help proofreading the pages. Kudos and endless thanks to Terry Thomas and Bonnie Crouse who went all out, handling the finances, calling chefs, answering emails, problem-solving, planning and much more--their talents and enthusiasm were irreplaceable.

Thank you also to Pam Stowe, Cindy Hoffman, Kathy McInerney, Shirley Mueller, Anne Athanassakis, Gerri French for parsing recipes and to my husband Paul Arganbright for his helpful suggestions and his support during the many long hours it took to bring this book to print. Most of all, thank you to Linda Blue, photographer extraordinaire who provided me with a wealth of gorgeous photos that make this cookbook of culinary delights a visual treat.

-Tama Takahashi, Editor and Cookbook Designer

Farm to Table, Sustainable, or Organic?

We want to be the company you call when it absolutely, positively has to be right.

I'm amazed at the innovation of chefs in our area and happy to live in a place where great thought and effort go into transforming local bounty.

I'm happy to live in a city with so much culinary experience and so many accomplished chefs who continually surprise us with new techniques, as well as their interpretation of classic dishes.

My hat's off the the Chefs showcased in this book and I offer a heartfelt "Thank You" for making our local food scene so strikingly unique.

There is no place I would rather call home than Santa Barbara California.

Bon Appetite,

Guy De Mangeon
The Berry Man, Inc.

THE BERRY MAN, INC.

205 West Montecito Street
Santa Barbara, CA 93101
www.theberryman.com
805.965.3772

We are deeply grateful to the amazing photographer, Linda Blue, recent winner of the 2013 News Press Reader's Choice Award for Photography.

Both our first and second editions of the Santa Barbara Culinary Arts cookbooks would not be the same without her talent. Linda has been a professional photographer for 20 years, creating striking photographs of food, weddings, portraits, events, wine country and more. Her clients include Touring & Tasting, California Cut Flower Commission, Los Arroyos, Laguna Blanca School, PizzaMizza, and Montecito Urban Farms.

Santa Barbara Culinary Arts has received rave reviews from our chefs and food purveyors on Linda's professionalism and engaging demeanor. Linda has been a true pleasure to work with and we thank her for her friendship, dedication and artistry.

Please visit: www.labluephotography.com for more examples of Linda's work.

LINDA BLUE PHOTOGRAPHY

www.labluephotography.com
Linda@labluephotography.com
805.962.6760

AZU
Seafood Paella
Recipe Courtesy Owner Laurel Moore

Servings: 4
Prep Time: 1 hour

Ingredients for the Seafood Paella:
8 ounces fish stock or clam juice
1/4 ounces saffron
1/4 ounce blended or extra virgin olive oil
4 ounces Arborio rice, uncooked
3 ounces white wine
2 ounces chorizo, diced small
2 1/2 ounces marinated artichoke hearts
1 ounce peas
3 ounces canned tomato
4 shrimp (size 20-25, large)
4 mussels
4 ounces calamari, cleaned and cut into rings
salt and pepper
lemon wedges
cilantro leaves for garnish

Directions for the Seafood Paella:
Bring the fish stock or clam juice to a boil. Pull off the heat and put the saffron in the broth and let sit for at least five minutes.

Put a quarter-sized amount of oil in a paella pan and place the pan over high heat. Add the Arborio rice and stir (wooden spoon works best) until the rice is toasted but not burnt. Turn down the heat (to prevent the alcohol from flaming up), add the white wine, then turn the heat back up.

After the wine cooks down, stir in the chorizo and cook until it starts releasing oil.

Add the saffron-infused stock 2 ounces at a time. When the rice is translucent on the ends, add the artichoke hearts, peas, tomato, shrimp, mussels, calamari and salt and pepper to taste. Add the last half of the stock and cook until the liquid has been absorbed by the rice.

Note: do not over stir the paella when adding the stock the second time so the rice cooks up crispy. Adjust seasoning to taste.

Suggested garnishes are lemon wedges and cilantro.

AZU

457 E Ojai Avenue
Ojai, CA 93023
Azuojai.com
Laureldmoore@gmail.com
805.284.4759

BACARA RESORT & SPA
Beef with Foie Gras and Onion
Recipe Courtesy Executive Chef Vincent Lesage

Servings: 4
Prep Time: 1 hour 30 minutes, plus overnight pickling

Ingredients for the Beef Foie Gras:
1 bunch mini red onion
1 cup verjus
2 cups sugar
3 cups water
1/2 cup pickling spice
1/2 lobe of foie gras
5 cups of milk
2 eggs
3 egg yolks
7 cups of heavy cream, in two parts
4 onions
4 ounces Parmigiano Reggiano cheese, grated
3 bunches of green onion
1 pound butter plus 2 teaspoons, in two parts
1/2 teaspoon salt
1 clove of garlic
1 handful of spinach
4 Black Angus rib eye steaks at 12 ounces each
1 black truffle

BACARA RESORT & SPA

8301 Hollister Avenue
Santa Barbara, CA 93117
www.bacararesort.com

844.887.9583

Directions for the Pickled Red Onions:
Clean and peel the mini red onions then cut in half. Bring the verjus, sugar, water and pickling spice to a boil, then pour over the onion in a non-reactive container and let marinate for 12 hours.

Directions for the Foie Gras Royale:
Preheat the oven to 250° F.

Cook foie gras in a pan then put it to rest on a plate with a napkin to absorb the fat. Warm up the milk in a small sauce pan. Pour into a blender and add the foie gras, eggs, egg yolks and 5 cups of the heavy cream then blend. Let sit for 30 minutes. Skim off the foam and spread the foie gras mixture in a sheet pan. Bake for 25 minutes. Let cool. Put in a blender and blend until a smooth consistency.

Directions for the Onion Puree:
Peel and slice the onions. Sweat them in a wide sauce pot in 2 teaspoons butter until all the liquid is evaporated. Caramelize the onions with the Parmesan cheese, add 2 cups of the heavy cream and cook for 15 minutes at low temperature. Let cool. Put the onion mixture into a blender and blend until a smooth consistency.

Directions for the Green Onion Foam:
Chop the green onion and put in a blender with 1 pound of butter, salt, garlic and spinach. Add boiling water equal to half the vollume of the mixture and blend for one minute. Strain and keep warm.

Directions for the Rib Eye:
Grill the ribeye steaks.

Reheat the Pickled Red Onion, Foie Gras Royale, Onion Puree and Green Onion mixture. Foam the green onion sauce with an immersion blender. Plate the ingredients and garnish with black truffle shavings.

BACARA RESORT & SPA
Sweet Yellow Corn Custard with Savory Granola, Crispy Kale, Avocado Emulsion, Aromatic Oil and Edible Flowers
Recipe Courtesy Chef de Cuisine Johan Denizot

Servings: 4
Prep time: 45 minutes, plus 4 hours chilling time

Ingredients for the Corn Custard:
2 cups fresh yellow corn juice
4 gelatin leaves, bloomed in ice water
2 egg yolks
zest of 1 lime
juice of 2 limes, in two parts
sea salt and freshly ground black pepper
Espelette pepper to taste
1 cup heavy cream
1 Hass avocado
1 tablespoon sour cream
1 1/8 teaspoon garlic, finely chopped
extra virgin olive oil
1 teaspoon chives, finely chopped
1/4 cup cooked lentils
1/4 cup oats
1 shallot, finely diced
1 teaspoon local Santa Barbara honey
(continued on right)

BACARA RESORT & SPA

8301 Hollister Avenue
Santa Barbara, CA 93117
www.bacararesort.com

844.887.9583

Ingredients for the Corn Custard (continued):
1 sprig of thyme
1/4 cup puffed wild rice
1 bunch Tuscan black kale
1 cup grape seed oil
8 scallions, only the green part
edible flowers

Directions for the Corn Custard:
Cut the kernels from the corn cobs and put the kernels through a juicer to extract the juice. Simmer the corn juice in a sauce pan until thickened, whisking continuously. Add the gelatin leaves, egg yolks, lime zest and juice of 1 lime, salt, black pepper and Espelette pepper to taste. Stir and cool down over an ice bath. Whisk the cream to a soft peak then season with salt and pepper. When the corn mixture is just barely set, fold in the heavy cream. Pour the custard into ramekins to 1/4 full. Let set for four hours in the refrigerator.

Directions for the Avocado Emulsion:
Peel the avocado and remove the seed. Cut the avocado in big chunks. Puree the avocado, sour cream, juice of 1 lime and garlic in a blender on high speed, adding 2 tablespoons oil slowly until emulsified. Transfer to a bowl and fold in the chives with a spatula. Season to taste with salt and pepper.

Directions for the Savory Granola:
Preheat the oven to 220° F.

In a bowl, mix together the cooked lentils, oats, shallot, honey, 2 tablespoons of oil and thyme. Spread the mixture on a sheet pan lined with parchment paper. Bake for 20 minutes, then remove from the oven and stir. Repeat until the mixture gets crispy. Fold in the puffed rice and let cool.

Directions for the Crispy Kale:
Wash the kale leaves and pat them dry. Cover a big plate with plastic wrap. Lay the kale leaves on top. Brush each leaf with oil and season with salt and pepper. Cook the kale leaves in the microwave on high for 2 minutes per batch until they are very crispy.

(continued on next page)

Photo by Linda Blue

BACARA RESORT & SPA
Sweet Yellow Corn Custard with Savory Granola, Crispy Kale, Avocado Emulsion, Aromatic Oil and Edible Flowers (cont.)

Recipe Courtesy Chef Johan Denizot

(continued from previous page)

Directions for the Aromatic Oil:

Wash and pat dry the scallions. Put them in a blender with the grape seed oil and puree on high for 3 minutes. Strain the puree through a chinois or strainer lined with cheesecloth.

Directions for Assembling the Dish:

Arrange the granola with a spoon in a little pile on top of the corn custard. With a pastry bag, form little kisses of avocado emulsion. Stick the crispy kale leaves inside the pudding vertically. Drizzle the aromatic oil and scatter the edible flowers around the dish.

CHEF DE CUISINE JOHAN DENIZOT

With an Italian mother, a French father and a resume that includes time in Switzerland and France, Chef de Cuisine Johan Denizot brings world-class experience to the Bacara Resort & Spa. At the age of 15, Chef Johan began his culinary journey at the Lycee Toussaint l'ouverture Culinary School in Pontarlier, France. He studied pastry and chocolate making before working in Lausanne, Switzerland and the French Alps.

Johan's first stop in the USA was Denver followed by San Francisco at Annabelle's Bar & Bistro. "I loved the diversity, the people and the creativity of San Francisco." says Johan. From there, he was introduced to Santa Barbara and the Santa Ynez Valley where he worked for two years in Valley kitchens before finding his place as the Chef de Cuisine at the Alisal Guest Ranch and then Root 246 where he worked alongside award-winning chef Bradley Ogden. Today, Johan adds his cosmopolitan influence to Bacara's award-winning dining experiences.

BACARA RESORT & SPA

EXECUTIVE CHEF VINCENT LESAGE

At the age of 30, Chef Vincent Lesage's impressive career already includes 3-Star Michelin restaurants in Paris as well as experience at some of the world's most luxurious hotels.

Born and raised in Paris at the center of the food universe, Lesage was surrounded by the rich flavors and techniques that define French gastronomy. But it was art that inspired him to become a chef. An avid art lover, he spent his spare time at the Louvre, studying the beautiful paintings and color palates that would later influence his artistic presentations.

After graduating from the Institut Paul Bocuse in Ecully, France, Lesage trained at some of the world's most celebrated establishments, including The Ritz Paris, the Michelin three-star restaurant, L'Astrance, and Michelin three-star restaurant, Bras.

Most recently, Lesage served as Executive Chef of Balboa Bay Resort in Newport Beach where he opened two of the city's only waterfront restaurants, Waterline and A&O Kitchen + Bar. Prior to that, he served as Executive Sous Chef at St. Regis Monarch Beach, managing a culinary team of more than 60.

Today, as Executive Chef of Bacara's renowned culinary program, Lesage oversees the resort's six dining experiences, including a new signature restaurant opening spring 2016.

When asked about his vision for Bacara, Lesage says "I approach every outlet as its own distinct concept. From a healthy breakfast at Spa Café to a casual family meal at The Bistro, each experience is unique, and each experience is exceptional."

When Lesage is not in the kitchen, he enjoys spending time with his family and exploring Santa Barbara's museums.

Photo by Linda Blue

BARBAREÑO
Popcorn Crème Brûlée
Recipe Courtesy Chef Julian Martinez

Servings: 6
Prep Time: 1 hour plus time to chill dessert

Ingredients for the Popcorn Crème Brûlée:
grape seed oil
100 grams raw popcorn kernels, preferably heirloom variety
950 grams heavy cream
Kosher salt
sugar (see recipe for amount)
egg yolks (see recipe for amount)

BARBAREÑO

205 W. Canon Perdido Street
Santa Barbara, CA 93101
www.barbareno.com
info@barbareno.com
805.963.9591

Directions for the Popcorn Crème Brûlée:
Pre-heat oven to 350° F. Set six 4-ounce ramekins in a deep baking pan.

Heat a generous amount of grape seed oil in a large pot on high heat until it just begins to smoke. Add the popcorn kernels, cover the pot and shake the pot a few times until you begin to hear the kernels begin to pop. Lower the heat to medium-high and cook, continuing to shake the pot often, until the popping slows to a trickle. Remove the pot from the heat and let stand covered for 1 minute. Uncover and discard any burnt kernels.

Bring the cream and a pinch of salt to a simmer. Add the popped popcorn and simmer for 30 seconds. Strain through a Chinois or cheesecloth-lined sieve. Bring the cream back to a simmer, then add the popcorn again. Cook for another 30 seconds, strain, and bring cream back to a simmer. Add the popcorn again and cook 30 seconds. Repeat this simmer-cook-strain process 8-10 times or until the cream has thickened considerably and tastes strongly of popcorn.

Weigh the strained popcorn cream. Divide that weight by 7.5, and add that amount of weight of sugar to the cream. Bring back to a light simmer to melt the sugar.

Meanwhile, separate the eggs. Use 1 large egg yolk per 125 grams of the cream. Place egg yolks in a bowl. Once the cream and sugar are hot, slowly add to the eggs, whisking constantly. Pour the mixture through a Chinois or cheesecloth-lined sieve and then divide evenly among the ramekins. Fill the baking dish with warm water to reach halfway up the sides of the ramekins. Cover pan tightly with aluminum foil and bake until the custards are just set but still slightly jiggly, about 30 minutes.

Transfer the ramekins to a cooling rack, then refrigerate until completely chilled. Just before serving, evenly sprinkle each custard with about 2 teaspoons of sugar. Caramelize with a kitchen torch until browned, being careful not to burn the sugar. Serve immediately.

BELLA VISTA at FOUR SEASONS THE BILTMORE SANTA BARBARA
Tagliatelle with Smoked Stone Crab, Uni, Chile, Garlic & Basil

Recipe Courtesy Executive Sous Chef Grant Macdonald

Servings: 4
Prep Time: 1 hour over the course of 2 days

Ingredients for the Homemade Tagliatelle:
1 pound durum semolina flour
1 pound all-purpose flour, plus extra for dusting
1.5 pounds egg yolks

Ingredients for the Smoked Stone Crab, Uni, Chile, Garlic & Basil:
1 whole stone or Dungeness crab (about 3 pounds)
1/2 pound applewood chips
3 cloves garlic, sliced
1 Fresno chile, thinly sliced
2 tablespoons butter, in two parts
1/2 cup white wine
1/2 tablespoon garum (or fish sauce)
1 1/2 pounds fresh tagliatelle (recipe below)
4 pieces uni
3 sprigs of basil, tops reserved for garnish, large leaves torn
1 tablespoon Parmegiano Reggiano, finely grated
salt to taste
2 tablespoons breadcrumbs, toasted

BELLA VISTA

1260 Channel Drive
Santa Barbara, CA 93108
www.fourseasons.com/santabarbara/dining/restaurants/bella_vista

805.969.2261

Directions for the Homemade Tagliatelle:
Using a stand mixer and paddle attachment, mix the flours and yolks together until fully combined, then continue to mix for 3 more minutes. Remove the dough from the mixer and knead into a ball. Flatten the dough using a pasta machine or rolling pin until it is thin enough to see the shape of your fingers through it. Dust with flour, and roll into a cylinder, then slice into 1/4" slices with a sharp knife. Dust with more flour, and toss gently with your fingers to separate the noodles. Let them dry on the counter for 30 minutes before using or freeze in a sealed container in small portions until you need them.

Directions for the Smoked Stone Crab, Uni, Chile, Garlic & Basil:
Prepare the crab the day before. Steam the crab for 10 minutes (20-25 minutes, if not smoking). Heat the applewood chips in a smoker until smoking, then hot smoke the crab for 15-20 minutes more at 225° F. Cool and reserve overnight in the refrigerator.

Pick the meat from the crab, reserving any juices. Discard gills and shells or save them for soup!

Sauté the garlic and Fresno chile in 1 tablespoon of butter, then deglaze with white wine. Add the fish sauce and reserved crab juice. Boil the fresh tagliatelle until al dente, then add to the pasta sauce, with a little of the pasta water. Reduce, stirring until there is only a few tablespoons of liquid left, then add the uni, smoked crab meat, 1 tablespoon of butter, basil leaves and cheese. Remove from the heat and stir briskly, until the sauce thickens. Dilute with a few drops more of pasta water if needed. Taste, season with salt and divide between 4 plates. Garnish with fresh basil tops and breadcrumbs.

Note: This dish celebrates two of the most delicious of our coastal delicacies, crab and uni. Smoking the crab is optional, but it adds an extra dimension to the dish. Garum is an Italian fish sauce made from mackerel or anchovies, but if you can't find it, Thai fish sauce is a good substitute.

We use fresh handmade pasta in the restaurant, but there are excellent dry tagliatelle available in stores that you can substitute, as you prefer.

BELMOND EL ENCANTO
Local Halibut Ceviche
Recipe Courtesy Chef Roberto Hernandez

Servings: 4
Prep Time: 30 minutes plus 3 hours marinating

Ingredients for the Local Halibut Ceviche:
1 pound halibut fillet
4 ounces cucumber (English recommended)
2 ounces jalapeño pepper
1/2 cup lemon juice, freshly squeezed
1/2 cup lime juice, freshly squeezed
1/4 cup orange juice, freshly squeezed
salt and pepper to taste
4 corn tortillas
canola oil
1 medium avocado
harissa spice
watermelon radish, thinly sliced, for garnish

Directions for the Local Halibut Ceviche:
Cut the fresh halibut into small strips, then set aside in a medium bowl. Thinly slice the cucumber and jalapeño, add to the halibut. Mix the lemon, lime and orange juices and combine with the halibut mixture. Add salt and pepper and combine well.

Cover the bowl with plastic wrap and place in the refrigerator for at least three hours for the mixture to cure.

Heat the canola oil in a pan to 350°F. Cut each tortilla into 16 pieces and add to the oil. Fry for 2-3 minutes or until the chips have reached the desired crispness. Season the chips with harissa spice to taste.

Peel and remove the pit from the avocado and divide into four parts. Slice each quarter to make an avocado "fan". Divide the ceviche between four dishes and garnish each with an avocado fan and fresh tortilla chips. The ceviche at right is plated on a bed of very thinly sliced watermelon radish.

BELMOND EL ENCANTO

800 Alvarado Place
Santa Barbara, CA 93103
www.belmond.com/elencanto

805.845.5800

Photo by Linda Blue

BOUCHON
Grilled Rack of Lamb with Eggplant, Rainbow Chard Sautée, Caramelized Onion, Farro Barley and Thai Basil Pesto

Recipe Courtesy Chef Chris Rossi

Servings: 4
Prep Time: 1 hour

Ingredients for the Grilled Rack of Lamb with Eggplant:
1 bunch Thai basil
1 cup olive oil, plus extra for sautéing
2 cloves garlic
1/4 cup pine nuts, toasted
Kosher salt
black pepper
2 tablespoons butter
1 large yellow onion, diced
1 cup farro
8 cups chicken stock
5 Japanese eggplant, sliced lengthwise, drizzled with olive oil
1 bunch rainbow chard, cleaned and hard vein removed, chiffonade into thin ribbons
2 racks of lamb (Frenched by butcher), eight bones each

BOUCHON

9 West Victoria Street
Santa Barbara, CA 93101
www.bouchonsantabarbara.com

805.730.1160

Directions for the Thai Basil Pesto:
Blanch the basil for one minute in hot water then place in ice water to cool. Remove and towel dry. In a food processor or blender, add the basil, 1 cup olive oil, garlic and pine nuts. Puree until smooth and season to taste with salt and pepper. Can be made up to 3 days ahead, keep refrigerated.

Directions for the Farro Barley:
In a medium sauce pan, heat 2 tablespoons butter. Sautée the onion until dark brown and caramelized. Add the farro and chicken stock and season with salt and pepper. Bring to boil and reduce to medium low. Cook uncovered for 35-40 minutes or until the farro is done. If there is excess liquid, strain farro. Keep warm until assembly.

Directions for the Eggplant and Rainbow Chard:
Grill eggplant for 3-4 minutes on each side then cut into 1 inch cubes. In a sauté pan, heat 2 tablespoons of olive oil, add the eggplant and rainbow chard. Sauté for 3 minutes or until chard is wilted. Season to taste with salt and pepper.

Directions for the Lamb:
Heat grill or barbeque on high. Heat oven to 400° F. Season lamb with salt and pepper. Place on grill and cook for 5 minutes on each side. Place lamb on a baking sheet and put into the preheated oven for 10 minutes. Take out and let rest for 10 minutes. Before serving, slice lamb between bones.

Directions to Assemble the Dish:
Place equal amounts of farro in the center of 4 plates, top with eggplant-chard sauté, arrange 4 bones from lamb around farro and vegetables, drizzle lamb generously with pesto.

Chef's Suggestion for Wine Pairing:
2012 Qupe Syrah, Bien Nacido Vineyard

Photo by Linda Blue

SORRISO ITALIANO
Uova Carbonara
Recipe Courtesy Chef Elisabetta Gerli

Servings: 6
Prep Time: 30 minutes

Ingredients for the Uova Carbonara:
1 red onion
1 tablespoon olive oil
1 tablespoon sugar
1 tablespoon wine vinegar
16 ounces bacon
5 ounces flour
6 yolks, at room temperature
salt
1 quart heavy whipping cream
1 cup Parmesan cheese

Directions for the Uova Carbonara:
Clean and slice the red onion then cook in a pan in the olive oil. When the onion starts to turn dark purple, add the sugar and vinegar together and continue cooking, stirring with a spoon until you see that the onions are caramelized. Set aside.

Dice the bacon and fry in a pan on the stove in its own grease.

Blend the flour, yolks and salt and set aside.

Heat the whipping cream in a deep pot until it starts bubbling. Add the hot cream to the flour/egg mixture, mixing carefully. Move the mix onto the stove again. Continue stirring until the mixture has thickened and will coat the back of a spoon.

In a bowl, layer the caramelized onion first, then add the cream and last the crispy bacon on top.

SORRISO ITALIANO

901 Embarcadero del Mar
Isla Vista, CA 93117
www.sorriso-italiano.com

805-324-4367

Photo by Linda Blue

THE STONEHOUSE at SAN YSIDRO RANCH
Grilled Marinated Spanish Octopus Salad
Recipe Courtesy Executive Chef Matt Johnson

Servings: 8
Prep Time: 3 1/2 hours, plus optional marinade overnight

Ingredients for the Marinated Octopus:
1 Spanish octopus
approximately 1 1/2 cups extra virgin olive oil
1 Vidalia onion, peeled and quartered
2 carrots, peeled
11 cloves garlic, smashed
3 stalks celery, roughly chopped
1/2 bottle Chardonnay
2 gallons vegetable stock or water
1 bunch parsley plus 3 tablespoons, chopped, in two parts
1 tablespoon red chile flakes
8 peppercorns
7 lemons, in three parts plus 1 tablespoon lemon juice
salt
2 oranges, juice and zest
6 cloves garlic, shaved
3 tablespoons oregano, chopped
3 tablespoons oregano, chopped
2 tablespoons scallion, chopped
2 tablespoons smoked Spanish paprika
1 tablespoons black pepper

THE STONEHOUSE at SAN YSIDRO RANCH

900 San Ysidro Lane
Santa Barbara, CA 93108
www.sanysidroranch.com
805.565.1700

Ingredients for the House Made Harissa:
1 tablespoon coriander
1 tablespoon caraway
1 tablespoon cumin
3 tablespoons extra virgin olive oil
1 red onion, diced
6 cloves garlic, smashed
1 quart piquillo peppers, roasted, peeled and seeded
1 tablespoon lemon juice
1 pinch crushed red pepper flakes
1 pinch powdered Espellete pepper

Ingredients for the Lemon Vinaigrette:	Other Ingredients:
juice of 2 lemons	pickled onion
1 tablespoon shallot, chopped	frisee
1 tablespoon Dijon mustard	raddichio
1 tablespoon honey	arugula
4 tablespoons Champagne vinegar	croutons
1 cup oil	sea salt

Directions for the Octopus:
Rinse the octopus thoroughly under cold water. Let sit under cold water. In a large hot stainless steel pot, add 1/4 cup oil, the onion, carrot, 11 cloves smashed garlic, and celery and sauté for about 15 minutes, until caramelized. Deglaze the pan with the wine and cook down until almost evaporated. Add the stock or water, 1 bunch parsley, chili flakes, peppercorns, lemon, 1/4 cup salt and another big drizzle of olive oil. When it comes to a boil, take the octopus with tongs and submerge it in the pot, then pull it out immediately. Do this about 4 times, until the tentacles turn up. Turn down the heat, put the octopus into the broth and simmer for 1 1/2 hours or until tender. Transfer it to an ice bath to cool. When cool, rub off the outside skin with a towel. Note: if you are not ready to marinade the octopus yet, let it rest in the refrigerator.

Cut the tentacles from the body there should be 8. Cut these into 3 pieces. Put in a large, non-reactive bowl with the juice, zest, 6 cloves shaved garlic, oregano, 3 tablespoons parsley, scallion, paprika, 1 tablespoon salt and pepper, mix well. Marinade for at least 4 hours. Overnight is better.

Directions continued on next page)

Photo by Linda Blue

THE STONEHOUSE at SAN YSIDRO RANCH
Grilled Marinated Spanish Octopus Salad (continued)

Recipe Courtesy Executive Chef Matt Johnson

(Directions continued from previous page)
Directions for the House Made Harissa:
Toast the coriander, caraway and cumin together in a dry pan. Sauté the onion and garlic until caramelized completely. Add the piquillo peppers and toasted spices and continue to cook. Blend the mixture in a blender, then finish with red pepper, Espellete pepper, 3 tablespoons of oil and the lemon juice.

Directions for Assembling the Octopus Salad:
Heat the grill. Add the octopus. Just char them and warm through because they are already cooked. Sauté the chorizo in 2 tablespoons of oil until caramelized. Transfer the chorizo to a mixing bowl. Reserve the oil from the pan. To the bowl, add the piquillo peppers that have been julienned, pickled onion, frisee, radicchio, arugula, chorizo, octopus, croutons and a little vinaigrette and sea salt. Mix well and taste for seasonings.

Spoon some harissa on each of the 8 plates. Top with equal parts of the salad mixture. Spoon a little of the chorizo oil left in the pan around it, adding a nice color to the plate. The harissa will last in the refrigerator for a week and is good with all sorts of dishes, especially lamb.

THE STONEHOUSE at SAN YSIDRO RANCH

900 San Ysidro Lane
Santa Barbara, CA 93108
www.sanysidroranch.com

805.565.1700

Located in a 19th-century citrus packing house, The Stonehouse features a relaxing lounge with full bar service and a separate dining room with crackling fireplace and creek side views. Guests can dine under the romantic gaze of Southern California's stars on the ocean view deck—a wood-burning fireplace and heated stone flooring provide year-round comfort. The Stonehouse regional cuisine is prepared with a palate of herbs and vegetables harvested from the on-site chef's garden.

Photo by Linda Blue

S.Y. KITCHEN
Zabaglione
Recipe Courtesy Chef Francesco Crestanelli

Servings: 6
Prep Time: 30 minutes

Ingredients for the Zabaglione:
1 1/2 cup sugar
1 cup Marsala, passito or other sweet wine
16 egg yolks
Panettone or Pandoro Italian sweet bread (optional) as side
fresh berries (optional) for garnish
shaved chocolate (optional) for garnish

Directions for the Zabaglione:
Mix the sugar, Marsala and egg yolks in a large bowl and whisk until sugar is incorporated and mixture is frothy, about 5-8 minutes.

Place over a pot of boiling water to create a double boiler and reduce heat to a simmer. Whip constantly until the custard becomes thick and creamy, taking care to not overheat or eggs will curdle.

Pour into serving glasses or custard cups and serve warm with some holiday Panettone or Pandoro.

Suggested garnishes are fresh berries or shaved chocolate.

S.Y. KITCHEN

1110 Faraday Street
Santa Ynez, CA 93460
www.sykitchen.com

805.691.9794

Photo by Linda Blue

BUCATINI
Gemelli alle Polpettine di Carmela
Recipe Courtesy Chef Raffaele Ferraro

Servings: 6
Prep Time: 1 hour

Ingredients for the Gemelli alle Polpettine di Carmela:
1 pound ground meat: 80% ground lean beef and 20% ground veal
3 ounces grated Parmesan cheese, plus extra for topping
1 egg
2 cloves garlic, one minced and one chopped, in two parts
1 ounce Italian parsley, chopped
salt and pepper to taste
1 ounce extra virgin olive oil
6 ounces mirepoix (equal mixture of roughly chopped celery, onions and carrots)
3 cups "San Marzano" chopped tomatoes
6 servings gemelli

Directions for the Gemelli alle Polpettine di Carmela:
Preheat oven to 350° F.

In large bowl, mix the ground meat, Parmesan cheese, egg, 1 minced clove of garlic, parsely and salt and pepper by hand. Form half-ounce balls and set evenly spaced apart on a baking sheet. Place in the oven for 45 minutes. Let cool for 15 minutes before placing in sauce.

Heat a large pan to medium heat. Add the extra virgin olive oil and 1 clove chopped garlic. Sauté garlic until golden, do not brown. Add the mirepoix and gently sauté until onions become translucent. Add the tomatoes and salt to taste.

Add the cooled meatballs to the sauce, cover, reduce heat to low and simmer for additional 15 minutes.

Cook the gemelli in salted boiling water for 8-10 minutes. Pasta should be 'al dente'. Drain, plate and top with meatballs and sauce. Sprinkle with grated Parmesan cheese and serve while hot.

Buon Appetito from our family to yours!

BUCATINI

436 State Street
Santa Barbara, CA 93101
www.bucatini.com

805.957.4177

Photo by Linda Blue

CA' DARIO
Gnocchi all Romana
Recipe Courtesy Chef Dario Furlati

Serves: 4-6
Prep Time: 30-40 minutes

Ingredients for the Gnocchi all Romana:
1 quart of milk
pinch salt
pinch nutmeg
7 ounces butter, in two parts plus extra for greasing pan
7 ounces semolina
2 egg yolks
7 ounces grated Parmesan, in two parts plus extra for garnish
sage leaves
black summer truffle (optional)

Directions for the Gnocchi all Romana:
Preheat the oven to 375° F.

Heat the milk with the salt, nutmeg and 3 ounces of the butter. Bring to a boil. Add the semolina by sprinkling the semolina over the top like rain while whisking to make sure no lumps are formed. Lower the temperature and cook for a few minutes while stirring continuously.

Once the mixture has thickened and is no longer watery, turn off the heat and add the egg yolks and 4 ounces of the grated Parmesan. Mix the dough for a few minutes to incorporate the ingredients.

Grease a rectangular pan with butter and spoon in the dough. Level with a spatula or a paper sheet to a depth of about 1 1/2". Cool for approximately 10 minutes.

Cut the dough into gnocchi with a 3-4" pasta cutter. Layer the gnocchi in a baking dish. Melt the other 4 ounces of butter. Cover the gnocchi with sage leaves, the melted butter and the rest of the Parmesan cheese. Bake for 20 minutes or until lightly brown.

Plate the gnocchi and dust with more Parmesan and shaved black truffle.

CA' DARIO

37 East Victoria Street
Santa Barbara, CA 93101
www.cadario.net

805.884.9419

Photo by Linda Blue

CECCO RISTORANTE
Oysters Fritti
with Sweet Pepper Agrodolce Sauce
Recipe Courtesy Chef David Cecchini

Serves: 3-4
Prep Time: 25 minutes

Ingredients for the Oysters Fritti:
2 red bell peppers, minced
1/4 cup garlic, minced
3 cups white balsamic vinegar
2 cups sugar
oil for deep frying
12 large oysters, shucked
3⁄4 cup cornstarch
1/4 cup flour
1 teaspoon baking powder
1/2 teaspoon salt
1/4 teaspoon pepper
1/4 cup cold sparkling water
1 egg, slightly beaten

Directions for the Sweet Pepper Agrodolce Sauce:
Combine the bell peppers, garlic, vinegar and sugar in a saucepan and reduce to a syrupy consistency.

Directions for the Cecco Oysters Fritti:
Preheat the oil in a deep fryer to 350° F.

Drain and pat dry the oysters. Mix the cornstarch, flour, baking powder, salt and pepper. Add the cold sparkling water and the egg to the dry mixture and mix gently just until it makes a slightly lumpy batter.

Dip oysters one at a time into the batter and fry until golden brown. Remove from fryer, drain and season with salt and pepper.

Serve hot with the Sweet Pepper Agrodolce Sauce.

CECCO RISTORANTE

475 1st Street #11
Solvang, CA 93463
www.ceccoristorante.com

805.688.8880

Photo by Linda Blue

C'EST CHEESE
Goat Grilled Cheese
Recipe Courtesy Chef Jamie Libardi

Servings: 4
Prep Time: 20 minutes

Ingredients for the Goat Grilled Cheese:
8 slices pullman loaf bread
4 3-ounce thin slice of Sierra Nevada Organic Monterey Jaques
4 3-ounce thin slice of Beemster Goat Gouda
1/4 pound Spanish chorizo, thinly sliced
4 Piquillo peppers, diced
4 ounces arugula
2 tablespoons butter

Directions for the Goat Grilled Cheese:
Butter one side of each slice of bread. Place four slices of the bread butter-side down on a cutting board and set the other four slices bread-side down.

Place a slice of each of the cheeses on top of the four slices that are butter-side down. Then, divide the chorizo, diced Piquillo pepper and arugula evenly between them. Put the four remaining slices of bread on top, butter-side up so the sandwich bread has butter on the outside top and bottom.

Place each sandwich on a hot flat top grill, panini grill or cast iron pan. Grill on one side until golden brown, then flip and grill until the cheese is melted.

Slice and serve. Careful—they are hot!! Enjoy!

C'EST CHEESE

825 Santa Barbara Street
Santa Barbara, CA 93101
www.cestcheese.com
info@cestcheese.com
805.965.0318

Started in 2003, C'est Cheese began as Santa Barbara's premier cheese shop and is now so much more! Having expanded in 2014, C'est Cheese is now a full cafe serving breakfast and lunch 7 days a week. We bake all our own pastries on site as well as roast our own meats, make our own jams and all sorts of other delicious things!

CHEF MICHELE MOLONY,
CHEF and COOKING INSTRUCTOR
Garden Market Salad
Recipe Courtesy Chef Michele Molony

Servings: 6
Prep Time: 1 hour 30 minutes

Ingredients for the Garden Market Salad:
1 pomegranate
1 shallot, minced
6 tablespoons lemon juice, in two parts
olive oil
salt
Santa Barbara County olive oil
1 firm Fuyu persimmon
1 delicata squash
one clove garlic
pinch red pepper flakes
1 bunch organic Tuscan kale

CHEF MICHELE MOLONY

chefmichelemolony.com
chefmichelemolony@gmail.com

805.895.4467

Directions for the Pomegranate Vinaigrette:
Make a paste with the garlic clove and a good pinch of salt. Scrape into a medium-sized bowl. Add the juice of 1/2 lemon [approximately 3 tablespoons], the red pepper flakes and 1/4 cup olive oil and whisk to combine.

Directions for the Garden Market Salad:
Preheat the oven to 375° F.

Cut the pomegranate in half and place into a bowl of cold water. Flick the seeds from the membranes with your fingertips--the seeds easily separate from the membranes underwater. Skim away the membranes as they float to the surface. Crush one third of the seeds in a small bowl with the shallot, 3 tablespoons lemon juice, a good pinch of salt and a splash of olive oil. Adjust seasoning to taste. Save the rest of the pomegranate seeds for garnish.

Slice the firm Fuyu persimmon as you would an apple, the thinner the slices the better. Stir into the pomegranate vinaigrette. Slice the delicata squash lengthwise and scoop out the seeds. Slice the squash into half moon shapes and toss in a small bowl with enough olive oil to coat them. Roast on a parchment-lined sheet pan for about thirty minutes or until tender and lightly caramelized.

Remove the tough inner ribs and stems from the kale. Stack the leaves and roll to form a loose bundle. Cut across the bundle of leaves to make a fine julienne. Put the kale into the bowl with the dressing and with the tips of your fingers massage the dressing into the kale. The lemon and salt will "cook" the kale, turning it into a sweet, green and healthy treat.

Directions for Assembling the Dish:
Squeeze out excess moisture from the wilted kale and spoon the kale onto a white platter. Gently layer on top the persimmons and delicata squash. Spoon the pomegranate vinaigrette over the salad and garnish with the pomegranate seeds. The salad is very good served at room temperature.

Note: The combination of Tuscan kale, Fuyu persimmon, pomegranate and delicata squash results in vibrant color and invigorating flavor.

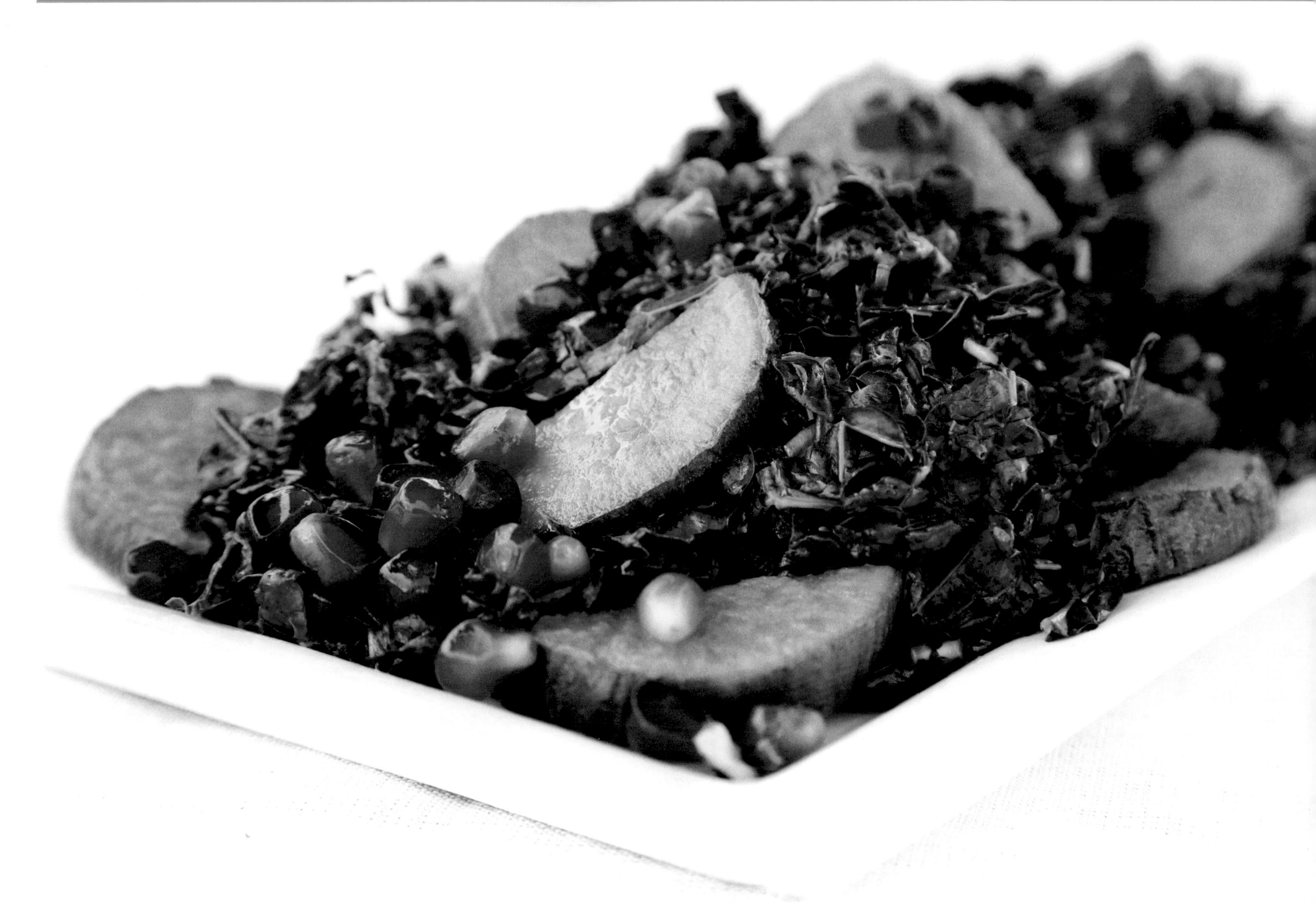

Photo by Linda Blue

CIELITO RESTAURANT AND TACQUERIA
Quinoa and Kale Fritters with Avocado Aioli, Mango Drizzle and Garnishes
Recipe Courtesy Executive Chef Kurt F. Steeber

Servings: 8
Prep Time: 1 hour, plus overnight pickling

Ingredients for the Quinoa and Kale Fritters:
4 ounces avocado meat
2 1/2 ounces grape seed oil, plus extra for frying
approximately 2 ounces of lime juice (1 fresh lime) plus extra
    to taste
1/2 ounce apple cider vinegar
2 cloves garlic, peeled and minced, in two parts
1/2 ounce cilantro leaves, chopped plus 5-6 sprigs for garnish
1/2 ounce basil, stemmed , washed and chopped
2 mangoes peeled and flesh removed
1/4 ounce Tabasco or hot sauce of your choice
1/4 teaspoon plus one pinch ancho chili powder, in two parts
1/8 teaspoon cayenne
Kosher salt
2 1/2 ounces quinoa
8 ounces vegetable stock or water
3 ounces white onion, peeled and minced
2 1/2 ounces sweet potato, peeled and small diced
1 egg
3/4 ounce flax seeds
3/4 ounce hemp seeds
 (continued on right)

CIELITO RESTAURANT AND TACQUERIA

1114 State Street
Santa Barbara, CA 93105
www.cielitoresturant.com
ksteeber@cielitoresturant.com
805.965.4770

Ingredients for the Quinoa and Kale Fritters (continued):
1/3 ounce Italian parsley, stemmed, washed and chopped
2 1/2 ounces green curly kale, stemmed, washed and chopped
1 1/4 ounces almond meal (substitute chickpea flour in case of nut
allergy)
1/2 ounce cornstarch
1/2 ounce ginger, peeled and minced
1 each radish, sliced thinly
1 each jalapeno, sliced thinly
5-6 sprigs of frisee lettuce

Directions for the Avocado Aioli:
Put the avocado, grape seed oil, 3/4 ounce lime juice, apple cider vinegar, 1 clove of minced garlic, cilantro and basil in a food processor or blender and pulse to puree. Remove with a rubber spatula, then set aside.

Directions for the Mango Drizzle:
Place the mangoes, 1 ounce lime juice, Tabasco, 1/4 teaspoon of the ancho chile and cayenne into a food processor and puree. Add salt to taste and set aside.

Directions for the Quinoa and Kale Fritters:
Rinse quinoa and dry in a towel. In a hot sauce pan, toast the quinoa in a film of oil until fragrant. Add the vegetable stock or water and bring to a boil. Reduce heat, cover and cook until liquid is absorbed, approximately 20 minutes.

Lightly sauté the onion and sweet potato in a small amount of oil until soft, then add the remaing clove of minced garlic.

In a large bowl, mix the egg, flax seeds, hemp seeds, parsley, kale, almond meal or chickpea flour, cornstarch, ginger and a pinch of ancho chile. Adjust seasoning to taste. Form batter into 1-ounce balls or patties. In a hot sauté pan, add grape seed oil to cover the bottom of the pan. Fry the fritters on all sides until browned. Reserve and cook remaining fritter batter.

Directions for Plating the Dish:
Pool avocado aioli in the center of each plate. Place 3 fritters in middle of the sauce on each plate. With a spoon, drizzle the mango sauce over the top. Toss the radish, jalapeno, frisée and cilantro together and season with lime juice and salt to taste. Use to garnish the fritters.

DEUX BAKERY
Peach Pie
Recipe Courtesy Chef Wendy Fleming

Servings: 6-8
Prep Time: 1 hour 35 minutes

Ingredients for the Peach Pie:
5 cups sliced yellow and/or white peaches (We used both because
    we had two trees in the backyard)
3 tablespoons lemon juice
2/3 cup sugar, plus extra for sprinkling
2 3/4 cup flour
1/2 pound cold butter, cut into cubes
scant 1/4 cup ice water
2 tablespoons cornstarch
1/2 teaspoon almond extract
1/2 teaspoon salt
egg wash or milk

Directions for the Crust:
Put the flour and butter in a food processor and mix for approximately 20 seconds. Pour the water into the top and mix until it comes together, about 10 to 15 seconds more. Roll out and line the bottom of a pie pan. Save the remaining dough for the top. Store in the refrigerator while you prepare the pie filling.

Directions for the Peach Pie:
Preheat the oven to 375° F.

In a large bowl, put in sliced peaches, lemon juice and sugar. Mix gently. Cover and let stand for at least an hour or overnight. Drain peaches, reserving juice. Depending on how long you let the peaches stand, you should have 1 to 2 cups juice.

Put the juice in a pan on the stove and let boil until it becomes syrupy, approximately 10 minutes. After the syrup has cooled for a minute or two, pour over the peaches. Add the cornstarch and almond extract. Stir gently.

Put the peach mixture in a prepared crust, cover with a lattice top or plain round top. Brush with egg wash or milk and sprinkle sugar on the crust.

Bake for 50 minutes. If the crust starts to brown too quickly, cover the pie with a vented piece of foil. Juices should look thick and bubbly around the rim and the pie should be boiling in the middle when done.

DEUX BAKERY

824 Reddick Street
Santa Barbara, CA 93103
www.deuxbakery.com
Chloe3277@me.com
805.770.3109

DINING WITH DI CATERING
Crab-Stuffed Piquillo Pepper Crostini
Recipe Courtesy Dining with Di
Adapted from Original by Half Baked Harvest

Servings: 4-6
Prep Time: 40 minutes

Ingredients for the Crab-Stuffed Piquillo Pepper Crostini :
1 egg yolk
1 tablespoon apple cider vinegar
1 tablespoon lemon juice
1 tablespoon smoked paprika
Kosher salt
1/2 cup olive oil, plus extra for brushing bread
2 tablespoons sriracha
black pepper
8 ounces deep sea red crab or lump crab meat
1 teaspoon Dijon mustard
2 tablespoons fresh cilantro, chopped
2 tablespoons red onion, diced
4 ounces Maytag blue cheese, in two parts
4 ounces jack cheese
cracked black pepper
1 jar (16 ounces) piquillo peppers, drained and patted dry (find in gourmet grocery stores)
1 baguette loaf, sliced thinly on diagonal

Directions for the Sriracha Aioli:
Whisk the egg yolk, apple cider vinegar and lemon juice in a large mixing bowl or Kitchen Aide® until creamy and pale (about 2 minutes). Add the smoked paprika and a pinch of salt; continue to whisk for another minute. When the mixture starts to thicken to the consistency of mayonnaise, slowly add the olive oil to the mixture one tablespoon at a time while whisking or whipping to incorporate the oil. Whisk in the sriracha, then salt and pepper to taste. The aioli should be thick and creamy in texture. Store in the refrigerator until ready to use.

Directions for the Crab-Stuffed Piquillo Peppers:
Preheat oven to 375°F.

In a bowl, add the crab meat, Dijon mustard, cilantro, red onions, 2 ounces of the blue cheese and the jack cheese. Mash all ingredients together with a spoon and season with Kosher salt and pepper.

Stuff the piquillo peppers with 1-2 tablespoons of filling. Place on a lightly greased baking sheet. Once all the peppers have been stuffed, bake for 15-20 minutes or until cheese begins to melt.

Remove peppers from oven and turn it on to broil. Place your baguette slices on a baking sheet and brush with olive oil, then season with salt and pepper. Place under the broiler for 1-2 minutes. (WATCH carefully!)

Remove from the oven and spread the remaining blue cheese on each slice. Place back in the oven for about 30 seconds and remove, then top with the stuffed peppers, drizzle with sriracha aioli, serve warm and enjoy!

DINING WITH DI CATERING

www.diningwithdi.com
www.diningwithdi.blogspot.com
diana@diningwithdi.com
https://instagram.com/diningwithdi

805-689-3111

Photo by Linda Blue

DOWNEY'S RESTAURANT
Red Rock Crab Salad with Papaya
Recipe Courtesy Chef John Downey

Servings: 6 for a light lunch
Prep Time: I hour plus 30 minutes if using fresh live crabs

Ingredients for the Fresh Ginger-Lime Dressing:
5 limes, in two parts
1/2 ounce fresh ginger, finely-grated
I teaspoon honey
I cup extra virgin olive oil
salt and pepper
dash of cayenne
3 whole fresh rock crabs or 12 large crab claws (available at the
    Saturday morning Fisherman's Market near the Breakwater)
I tablespoon pickling spices
1/4 cup cider vinegar
2 ripe Hawaiian papayas
I ounce pine nuts, toasted
fresh basil (green, opal or both), finely shredded

Directions for the Fresh Ginger-Lime Dressing:
Zest I lime. Squeeze it, along with another lime, to fill a 1/4 cup measuring cup. Combine the zest, lime juice, ginger, honey and oil. Let stand for 30 minutes. Season to taste with salt, pepper and cayenne and use as needed.

Note: Dressing can be used with this crab salad or watercress and fresh strawberries.

Directions for the Crab Salad:
Cook the crabs by placing them in a large pot of cold water which has been seasoned with 2 tablespoons salt, pickling spices and cider vinegar. The crabs may try to escape so quickly cover the pot with a weighted lid and bring it just to a boil. Remove the crab from the pot and cool under cold running water. Refrigerate until you are ready to use.

To clean the crab, remove each of the claws and legs. Discard the body as the very little amount of meat inside is difficult to remove. This can be a messy job so be sure to do it over the sink! Crack the claws and the larger sections of the legs with a mallet or the back of a heavy knife. Pick out the crab meat being sure to remove all pieces of shell. Set meat aside in refrigerator. If you prefer, you may find freshly picked Dungeness crab meat at local fine seafood purveyors such as Santa Barbara Fish Market. Allow 3 ounces crab meat per person.

Peel 2 limes using a small sharp knife. Remove all zest and white pith. Cut out the segments carefully and set aside.

Peel the papayas using a vegetable peeler, cut in half and remove the seeds. Cut into thick slices and arrange on six plates.

Divide the crab among the plates, garnish with a sprinkling of toasted pine nuts, a little finely-shredded basil, and the lime segments then splash the lime-ginger dressing lightly on top.

Enjoy with a nice Santa Barbara Chardonnay.

DOWNEY'S RESTAURANT

1305 State Street
Santa Barbara, CA 93101
www.downeyssb.com

805.966.5006

Photo by Linda Blue

DUO CATERING
Nori and Miso Roasted Black Cod with Radish and Citrus Salad

Recipe Courtesy Chef Brian Congdon
and Chef Ashley Transki

Servings: 6
Prep Time: 15 minutes

2 pounds black cod fillets, skin removed, cut into 6 portions
    approximately 5 ounces each
salt and pepper
4 sheets of dry roasted nori, finely chopped
1/2 cup white [Shiro] miso paste
1 teaspoon fresh ginger, minced
1 teaspoon coriander seeds, toasted and crushed
juice and zest of one lemon
1 tablespoon + 1 teaspoon sesame oil, in two parts
1 tablespoon Duo Sweet Chili Sauce (a store bought chili sauce
    can be substituted)
8 French breakfast radishes, thinly sliced on a mandolin
6 kumquats, thinly sliced into rounds
2 sprigs mint, stems removed
2 sprigs cilantro, stems removed
1 teaspoon unseasoned rice wine vinegar
pinch of flaked salt (Maldon or similar)

Directions for the Nori and Miso Roasted Black Cod :
Preheat the oven to 400° F.

Season cod with salt and pepper, set aside. Combine the nori, miso, ginger, coriander, lemon juice and zest, 1 tablespoon sesame oil, and Duo Sweet Chili Sauce in a small bowl, mixing with the back of a wooden spoon until a paste forms.

Spread 1 tablespoon of the paste onto each fillet.

Roast in the oven for 8-10 minutes.

Gently toss the radish, kumquats, mint, cilantro, rice wine vinegar and salt together. Spoon over the fish once it has been removed from the oven.

Serve with rice and gingered broccolini.

DUO CATERING

614 East Haley Street
Santa Barbara, CA 93103
www.duoevents.com
info@duoevents.com
805.957.1670

FINCH & FORK at the CANARY HOTEL
Smoked Trout and Olive Deviled Eggs
Recipe Courtesy Executive Chef James Siao

Servings: 12
Prep time: 45 minutes, plus overnight marinating shallots

Ingredients for the Pickled Shallots:
6 large shallots, peeled
1 cup distilled vinegar
1/4 cup sugar
1 tablespoon salt
1/2 tablespoon mustard seeds
1/2 teaspoon whole coriander
1 teaspoon black peppercorn

Ingredients for the Smoked Trout and Olive Deviled Eggs:
12 eggs
1/3 cup mayonnaise
2 tablespoons Dijon mustard
1 tablespoon whole grain mustard
3 dashes Tabasco sauce
1 tablespoon Worcestershire sauce
2 teaspoons + 2 tablespoons chives, finely chopped, in two parts
salt and pepper to taste
6 ounces smoked trout (or other smoked fish)
4 tablespoons olive relish (Castelventrano and Kalamata olives
    chopped and blended with lemon zest and olive oil)
4 tablespoons pickled shallots

Directions for the Pickled Shallots:
Slice shallots into thin rings and place in medium bowl. In a small pot combine the vinegar, sugar, salt, mustard seeds, coriander and peppercorns and bring to boil until the sugar is dissolved. Then pour over shallots and place a plate on top to submerge them and let cool to room temp. When cool, refrigerate a few hours or overnight covered with plastic wrap or in a sealed container.

Directions for the Smoked Trout and Olive Deviled Eggs:
Bring a large pot of water to boil, gently place the eggs in boiling water and cook for 11 minutes. Transfer eggs to ice bath to cool. Shell eggs, cut in half and separate yolks.

Place the yolks, mayonnaise, mustard, Tabasco, Worcestershire and 2 teaspoons chopped chives in a bowl and whisk until well blended. Add salt and pepper to taste.

Place yolk mixture into a piping bag and fill each egg white half to the top.

Directions to Garnish the Eggs:
Top with a little olive relish, pieces of smoked trout, a couple pickled shallot rings, and the remaining chopped chives.

FINCH & FORK at the CANARY HOTEL

31 West Carrillo Street
Santa Barbara, CA 93101
www.finchandforkrestaurant.com

805-879-9100

FIRE & WINE WOOD FIRED CATERING
Fig and Candied Walnut Pizza
Recipe Courtesy Chefs Gretchen and Chris Rogers

Servings: 2 pizzas
Prep Time: 1 hour 20 minutes - 2 hours 20 minutes

Ingredients for the Fig and Candied Walnut Pizza:
1 cup dried figs
3 cups red wine, plus extra if needed
1/2 cup + 3 tablespoons granulated sugar, in two parts
1/4 teaspoon of cinnamon
2 tablespoons of lemon juice
coarse salt
1 cup walnuts
3 tablespoons olive oil
1 teaspoon fresh rosemary, finely chopped
pinch red pepper flakes
2 8- to 10-inch rounds store-bought pizza dough
approximately 1/8 cup flour
2 slices bacon, cooked and chopped
1/8 cup blue cheese, crumbled
8 slices fresh Mozzarella
2 cups arugula
4 fresh figs, sliced (optional)

Directions for the Fig Puree:
Combine dried figs, wine, 1/2 cup sugar, cinnamon, lemon juice and a pinch of salt and cook on stovetop over medium heat for 1-2 hours reducing and adding more wine as needed. Reduce until the figs are plump and the liquid is syrupy. Remove from the heat, set aside to cool to room temperature and puree in food processor. This will be the pizza "sauce".

Directions for the Walnuts:
Preheat the oven to 350° F.

Combine the walnuts, olive oil, 3 tablespoons sugar, 2 teaspoons salt, rosemary and pepper flakes and bake on a parchment-lined sheet pan for 15-20 minutes.

Directions for the Fig and Candied Walnut Pizza:
Preheat the oven to the highest possible temperature with the pizza stone inside.

Put the pizza dough in a glass bowl, cover with plastic wrap and let sit until it reaches room temperature. Using extra flour to prevent sticking, stretch dough into the desired shape and place on a floured pizza peel.

Spread fig puree, sprinkle chopped bacon and crumbled blue cheese, place mozzarella onto pizza and transfer onto pizza stone. Bake in oven for 10-15 minutes or until it reaches the desired crispiness. Remove from the oven, cut into slices, top with fresh arugula and the candied walnuts. Finish with optional fresh fig slices.

FIRE & WINE WOOD FIRED CATERING

P.O. Box 553
Los Olivos, CA 93441
www.fireandwinecatering.com
fireandwinecatering@gmail.com

805.680.0898

FOLEY FOOD & WINE SOCIETY
CHALK HILL - Citrus-Cured and Broiled Black Cod with Green Herb Sauce

Recipe Courtesy Executive Chef Ryan Freebern

Servings: 4
Prep Time: 2 hour 45 minutes, including 2 hour curing time

Ingredients for the Citrus-Cured and Broiled Black Cod:
1 - 1 1/2 pound black cod (sablefish) fillet
1 tablespoon Kosher salt, plus extra for seasoning
1 tablespoon sugar
1/2 teaspoon lemon zest
1/2 teaspoon lime zest
1 teaspoon + 1/2 cup fresh Italian parsley, chopped, in two parts
1/2 teaspoon + 2 tablespoons fresh thyme, chopped, in two parts
1 cup good white wine
1 cup water
1/4 cup shallots, very thinly sliced
1 clove garlic, crushed, chopped
1/2 teaspoon black peppercorn, cracked
cooking oil
1/2 cup fresh Italian parsley leaves
1/4 cup fresh tarragon leaves
1/4 cup fresh chives
2 tablespoons fresh fennel tops (optional)
2 - 4 tablespoons butter, room temperature

Directions for the Citrus-Cured and Broiled Black Cod:
Skin and portion the fillet into 4 servings. Use large tail section of black cod if available. If using a whole fillet, the pin bones can either be cut out, or left in and removed with tweezers after cooking. Place portions in a pan and set aside.

In a small bowl, combine 1 tablespoon salt and the sugar. Add the lemon zest, lime zest, 1 teaspoon of the parsley, and 1/2 teaspoon of the thyme. Mix and immediately apply to the fish, sprinkling lightly on all sides. (You may not need to use all of the curing mixture.) Refrigerate fish for two to three hours.

While the fish is curing, combine the wine, water, shallot, garlic, and pepper in a small saucepan. Bring to a boil, and reduce by half. Set aside.

Preheat the broiler with the rack to the top position. Remove the fish from the refrigerator and allow to temper for about 15-20 minutes. Line a sheet tray or broiler pan with aluminum foil, dull side up, and brush lightly with cooking oil. Using your hands, wipe most of the herbs and zest from the fish, then place fish on the lined pan.

Reheat the wine reduction until it begins to simmer. Add to a blender with the remaining 1/2 cup parsley, tarragon leaves, chives, fennel (optional) and butter. Puree until the mixture is smooth. Adjust seasoning to taste with salt.

Put the fish in the broiler for 2-4 minutes. Remove fish from broiler when it is lightly caramelized and beginning to show its flake. Serve immediately with the green herb sauce.

Paired perfectly with the Lincourt 2013 Steel Chardonnay.
The secret to our success with our Steel Chardonnay has been the high quality of fruit from our estate vineyard. Our 2013 Steel Chardonnay opens with fresh tangerine zest and citrus on the nose. Flavors of candied lemon and meringue are complemented by soft notes of flint and kumquat for a clean and refreshing finish.

FOLEY FOOD & WINE SOCIETY

Bacara Resort & Spa, 8301 Hollister Avenue
Santa Barbara, CA 93117
www.foleyfoodandwinesociety.com/Wineries/Central-Coast/
Foley-Food-and-Wine-Society-Tasting-Room-at-Bacara

805.968.1614

FOLEY FOOD & WINE SOCIETY
CHALK HILL
Pork Tenderloin, Sweet Corn Polenta
Recipe Courtesy Executive Chef Ryan Freebern

Servings: 4
Prep Time: 1 hour 30 minutes, including 1 hour tempering

Having worked with some of the most highly acclaimed chefs in San Francisco, Chalk Hill Estate's Executive Chef Ryan Freebern is one of wine country's elite culinary masters.

For more than a century, the Chalk Hill land has been an important producer of gourmet produce, meats, poultry and wine. Our organic garden delivers fresh and varied heirloom cultivars to the Chalk Hill kitchen year-round. When promoted to Executive at Chalk Hill, Chef Ryan stated, "The ability to work with the wonderful produce here at Chalk Hill is truly an inspiring gift."

Ingredients for the Pork Tenderloin:
1 1/4 pound pork tenderloin, cleaned of excess fat and silverskin
Kosher salt
1 teaspoon black peppercorns, plus extra for seasoning
1 teaspoon fennel seed
1/4 teaspoon crushed red pepper flake
1 teaspoon paprika
1 tablespoon Italian parsley, chopped
1 teaspoon fresh thyme, chopped
1 clove garlic, minced
(continued on right)

FOLEY FOOD & WINE SOCIETY

Bacara Resort & Spa, 8301 Hollister Avenue
Santa Barbara, CA 93117
www.foleyfoodandwinesociety.com/Wineries/Central-Coast/
Foley-Food-and-Wine-Society-Tasting-Room-at-Bacara
805.968.1614

Ingredients (continued from left):
zest of 1 lemon, minced
2 tablespoons extra virgin olive oil, plus more for cooking
2 ears sweet white corn, shucked and cleaned of silk
2-3 tablespoons butter, room temperature
1/4 cup Parmigiano Reggiano or Pecorino Romano, finely grated

Directions for the Pork Tenderloin:
An hour before cooking, remove the pork tenderloin from the fridge, unwrap, season liberally with salt and allow to temper on a rack over a pan. In a small pan over medium heat, lightly toast the peppercorns and fennel until fragrant, remove from heat, add in red pepper, toss for 30 seconds, then put spices into a grinder and pulse until spices are ground.

Combine spice mixture with paprika, parsley, thyme, minced garlic and lemon zest. Rub this mixture over the tenderloin, then truss and coat with the olive oil. (You can fold the tail under the tenderloin and truss to help create a more regular shape for even cooking.) Allow to continue tempering for the hour. Preheat your oven to 375 ° F.

Using the large holes of a box grater, grate the kernels from the ears of corn, removing as much of the milk as you can. Put into a small to medium non-stick sauce pan.

When ready, heat a skillet over medium-high heat. When hot, add the oil. When the oil shimmers and begins to smoke, add the pork and sear on all sides. Put pork on a baking tray and bake for 8-12 minutes depending on size. (Use an oven safe probe to precisely reach your ideal temperature for doneness.) Remove from oven and allow to rest 10-15 minutes before removing the trussing and slicing.

When the pork goes in the oven, heat the sweet corn over medium high heat, stirring frequently to avoid clumping. Allow to come to a boil, stirring continuously until polenta thickens, about 1-2 minutes. Remove from heat, stir in butter and grated cheese to finish. Adjust seasoning.

Paired perfectly with the Chalk Hill 2012 Pinot Noir.
This Pinot shows the ripe, sunny richness boasting a dark ruby/purple color as well as a beautiful bouquet of violets, raspberries, blueberries and black cherries.

FRESCO FIVE POINTS CAFE'
Rice and Parmesan Croquettes with Romesco Sauce
Recipe Courtesy Chef/Owner Mark Brouillard

Servings: 4
Prep Time: 1 hour

Ingredients for the Rice and Parmesan Croquettes with Romesco Sauce:
1 large red bell pepper, roasted
1 garlic clove, chopped
1/2 cup slivered almonds, toasted
2 tomatoes, roasted
2 tablespoons leaf parsley, chopped
2 tablespoons sherry vinegar
1 teaspoon smoked paprika
1/4 cup + 2 tablespoons extra virgin olive oil, in two parts
pinch of salt
1 small onion finely chopped
2 cups Arborio rice
2 cups chicken stock
1/4 teaspoon saffron threads, crumbled
2 tablespoons unsalted butter
2 1/4 teaspoon salt
1 small fresh tomato, chopped fine
1/2 cup fresh or frozen baby peas
1/4 cup dry white wine
(continued at right)

Ingredients (continued from left):
1 tablespoon rosemary, finely chopped
1/2 teaspoon ground black pepper
2 cups Parmesan cheese
2 large eggs
4 cups panko breadcrumbs
vegetable oil

Directions for the Romesco Sauce:
Blend the bell pepper, garlic, almonds, tomatoes, parsley, sherry vinegar, paprika and 1/4 cup olive oil until smooth. Season with a pinch of salt to taste.

Directions for the Croquettes:
Heat 2 tablespoons olive oil in a large heavy saucepan and add the onions and sauté lightly. Add the rice and sauté a few minutes, add the chicken stock, saffron and butter. Cook until the liquid is reduced by half, then add tomato, peas, wine, fresh rosemary and pepper. Cook until all the liquid is absorbed, then add the Parmesan and eggs and stir until mixed.

Spread out on a sheet pan and cool completely. Roll into tablespoon-sized balls and coat with panko crumbs. Deep fry in canola oil or vegetable oil until browned. Serve with the Romesco sauce.

FRESCO FIVE POINTS CAFE'

3987 State Street
Santa Barbara, CA 93105
www.frescosb.com

805.966.5006

HITCHING POST II
Grilled Pasilla Pepper Stuffed with Spot Prawns and Provolone

Recipe Courtesy Chef Frank Ostini

Servings: 4
Prep Time: 45 minutes

Ingredients for the Grilled Pasilla Pepper Stuffed with Spot Prawns and Provolone with Corn Salsa:
2 ears of corn, shucked,
2 tablespoons + 1 ounce butter, melted, in two parts
2 tablespoons + 2 ounces lemon juice, in two parts
salt and freshly ground black pepper
1/4 bunch cilantro
4 tablespoons olive oil, in two parts
2 tablespoons white wine vinegar
2 tablespoons lime juice
1/4 jalapeno, seeded, chopped
1 garlic clove
1 tablespoon green onion, chopped
1 teaspoon fresh ginger, minced
1/4 red onion, diced
1/2 red bell pepper, diced
4 Santa Barbara spot prawns (or 8 Channel or Gulf Shrimp)
2 ounces white wine
4 pasilla peppers
8 1-ounce slices Provolone cheese

HITCHING POST II

406 East Highway 246
Buellton, CA 93427
www.hitchingpost2.com

805.688.0676

Directions for the Corn Salsa:
Baste corn in a mixture of 2 tablespoons butter, 2 tablespoons lemon juice and salt and pepper to taste. Grill on the barbeque. Remove before fully cooked. Cut kernels off cob and reserve in a mixing bowl.

Mix the cilantro. 2 tablespoons olive oil, the vinegar, lime juice, jalapeno, garlic clove and green onion in a blender or food processor. Season to taste with salt and pepper.

Sauté the ginger and red onion in 2 tablespoons olive oil for 3 minutes over medium heat. Add red pepper and the previously prepared corn, then cook 2 minutes or until warm. Place warmed corn mixture in a salad bowl and toss with dressing until well combined. May be served warm or room temperature and prepared in advance. Store in airtight container in refrigerator until ready to serve.

Directions for the Prawns and Grilled Peppers:
Remove shells and devein prawns. Skewer and marinate in a mixture of 1 ounce melted butter, white wine and 2 ounces of lemon juice for 15 minutes. Grill on the barbeque over medium heat for 2-3 minutes per side or until just opaque. Remove from heat and reserve.

Fire roast the peppers over very hot barbeque fire or on a gas stove top. Allow the pepper skin to burn to black char. Remove peppers from heat then cover them for 15 minutes to cool. Peel and discard the burnt skin from peppers. Slit open each pepper to clean away seeds and the inside rib fibers.

Slice each prawn lengthwise. Place 2 ounces of cheese and 1 slice of shrimp in the cavity of each pepper. Let the stuffed peppers marinate for 15 minutes in the butter/white wine/lemon mixture. Grill the peppers on hot barbeque until the cheese is melted. Serve with the corn salsa.

Photo by Linda Blue

HUNGRY CAT
Chorizo and Clams
Recipe Courtesy Chef David Lentz

Servings: 4
Prep Time: 2 hours, plus overnight softening

Ingredients for the Garbanzo Beans:
1 1/2 cups dried garbanzo beans
extra virgin olive oil
2 quarts white onion, diced, in three parts
6 cloves + 1 pint garlic, thinly sliced, in three parts
4 chile de árbol pepper, in three parts
3 sprigs rosemary, in three parts
salt and pepper
1 quart red bell pepper, chopped
2 quarts sherry
1 tablespoon smoked paprika
1 tablespoon hot paprika
1 bunch Tuscan black kale
1 1/2 cup soft Mexican chorizo
60 Manila clams
1 quart sherry
2 cups chicken stock
2 tablespoons butter
juice of 1/2 a lemon
1 tablespoon parsley, chopped
2 tablespoons aioli
4 thick slices of bread, grilled

HUNGRY CAT

1134 Chapala Street
Santa Barbara, CA 93101
www.thehungrycat.com/santa_barbara.html

805.884.4701

Directions for the Garbanzo Beans:
Soak the dried garbanzo beans overnight. Heat 3 tablespoons olive oil in a heavy-gauge saucepan and sweat 1 pint of the onion, 3 cloves of the garlic, 1 chile de árbol and 1 sprig of the rosemary. Add the garbanzo beans and water or stock to cover. Simmer until soft and season to taste with salt and pepper.

Directions for the Sofrito:
In a heavy-gauge pot, heat 3 tablespoons olive oil and add the remaining 2 chile de árbol and 1 sprig rosemary. Cook for 1 minute then add the 1 quart onions, 1 pint garlic and the bell pepper and sweat until translucent. Add the sherry and reduce until dry. Add the smoked paprika and the hot paprika, season to taste with salt and pepper, then stir in 1 1/2 cups olive oil. Cook over low heat for 2 hours.

Directions for the Kale
Remove the ribs from the kale leaves then blanch them in salted boiling water. Remove, then squeeze all the water out. In a heavy-gauge pot, add 6 tablespoons olive oil, 1 chile de árbol, and 1 sprig rosemary. Add the 1 pint onion and 3 cloves garlic and cook until translucent. Add the kale and braise over low heat, adding oil as needed if the kale gets too dry. Cook for about an hour until the kale is very soft. Season to taste with salt and pepper.

Directions for the Chorizo and Clams:
Heat a heavy-gauge sauce pan over medium heat. Add the chorizo and render until it is cooked. Stir in 1 cup of the soffrito,. Add the garbanzo beans, kale and clams and deglaze with sherry. Cover and cook about 3-4 minutes for the clams to open. Add the chicken stock and butter and reduce the heat. Season with salt and pepper, add lemon juice and taste for seasoning. Finish with parsley.

Serve in a bowl with a generous spoon of aioli on top and the grilled toast.

IL FUSTINO
Cumin-and-Coriander Grilled Lamb Ribs

Recipe Courtesy Chef James R. Kirkley IV

Servings: 4
Prep Time: 2 hours 50 minutes

Ingredients for the Cumin-and-Coriander-Grilled Lamb Ribs:
1/4 cup Kosher salt
2 tablespoons light brown sugar
1 tablespoon ground cumin
1 tablespoon ground coriander
1 teaspoon freshly ground pepper
1/2 teaspoon ground cinnamon
Two 2 1/2 to 3-pound racks of lamb ribs
1 cup il Fustino Pomegranate Vinegar
2 tablespoons molasses

Directions for the Cumin-and-Coriander-Grilled Lamb Ribs:
In a bowl, mix the salt, sugar, cumin, coriander, pepper and cinnamon. Transfer 2 tablespoons of the rub to a medium bowl. In a large, shallow baking dish, sprinkle the remaining rub over the lamb ribs, massaging it into the meat. Let stand at room temperature for 1 hour.

Heat a gas grill. Whisk together the pomegranate vinegar, molasses and reserved 2 tablespoons of rub.

Place the lamb ribs, meaty side down, on the grill. Cook over moderately low heat, turning once, until lightly charred all over, 7 to 10 minutes. Reduce the heat to low and grill, turning and basting with the sauce every 10 minutes, until the meat is very tender and nicely charred, 1 hour and 30 minutes. Transfer the ribs to a carving board, tent with foil and let rest for 10 minutes. Cut the ribs between the bones and serve.

Note: This recipe combines the sweet and tangy flavor of American barbeque with Middle Eastern seasonings like pomegranate, and molasses.

IL FUSTINO, OILS AND VINEGARS

3401 State Street and 38 West Victoria
Santa Barbara, CA
www.ilfustino.com

888.798.4740

Photo by Tama Takahashi

JANE RESTAURANT
MONTECITO CAFE'
Fresh Mixed Seafood and Vegetable Stew
Recipe Courtesy Chef Mark Huston

Servings: 2
Prep Time: 30 minutes

Ingredients for Fresh Mixed Seafood and Vegetable Stew:
1/2 cup fresh seasonal vegetable, blanched and chilled ahead
1/4 cup new potatoes, chopped and blanched
1/4 teaspoon fresh garlic, chopped
1/4 teaspoon fresh ginger, chopped
1/4 teaspoon fresh jalapenos, chopped
8 ounces coconut milk
4 ounces fresh and cleaned black mussels
5 ounces fresh and cleaned Manila clams
3 each fresh and cleaned black shrimp
2 1/2 ounces fresh bay scallops
3 ounces fresh seasonal fish, roughly chopped into medium-sized
   pieces
1/2 cup fresh spinach
1/4 cup fresh chopped tomatoes
2 ounces white wine
garlic salt and pepper to taste
Italian parsley, chopped for garnish

Directions for Fresh Mixed Seafood and Vegetable Stew:
Blanch fresh seasonal vegetables and chill. Chop and blanch new potatoes.

Over medium to high heat, combine garlic, ginger jalapeno, new potatoes and coconut milk in a deep sauté pan or Dutch Oven. Add mussels and clams and bring to a boil.

After the mixture has reached a boil, add the shrimp, bay scallops, fresh fish, spinach, tomatoes and blanched vegetables. Season with white wine, garlic salt and pepper to taste.

Once the seafood has cooked and shells have opened divide into 2 bowls. Garnish with chopped Italian parsley and serve.

JANE RESTAURANT

1311 State Street
Santa Barbara, CA 93101
www.janerestaurantsb.com

805.962.1311

MONTECITO CAFE'

1295 Coast Village Road
Montecito, CA 93108
www.montecitocafe.com

805.969.3392

Photo by Linda Blue

THE LARK
Roasted Beet Salad with Toasted Pistachios, Strawberries, Burrata, Frisée and Hibiscus Vinaigrette

Recipe Courtesy Executive Chef Jason Paluska

Servings: 4
Prep Time: 1 hour 10 minutes

Ingredients for the Roasted Beet Salad:
1 pound beets, cleaned, with skin on
Kosher salt
freshly ground black peppercorn
3 ounces + 2 cups extra virgin olive oil, in two parts
3 ounces + 2 1/2 cups red wine vinegar, in two parts
1 bunch of fresh thyme
1 teaspoon whole black peppercorns
1 teaspoon juniper berries
2 each bay leaves
1 cup dried hibiscus (available at specialty grocers and Trader Joe's)
1 cup sugar
1 vanilla bean, split
2 cups olive oil
1/4 pound burrata, sliced into 4 portions
4 strawberries, sliced
6 ounces pistachios, toasted
4 ounces frisée and mache greens, cleaned

THE LARK

131 Anacapa Street
Santa Barbara, CA 93101
www.thelarksb.com

805.284.0370

Directions for the Roasted Beets:
Preheat the oven to 350° F.

Combine the beets, 1/2 ounce salt, 1/2 ounce freshly ground black peppercorn, 3 ounces extra virgin olive oil, 3 ounces vinegar and thyme in a mixing bowl to coat the beets evenly. Place into a 10" x 12" baking dish that is deep enough to contain the beets. Pour enough water into the dish to submerge the bottom 1" of the beets (approximately 6 ounces). This will help the beets from scorching. Wrap the baking dish in foil; this will ensure that the beets will steam as well as bake evenly. Place into the oven and cook for 45 minutes to an hour, depending on size of the beets. Remove when knife-tender. Add remaining water if needed throughout the cooking process so that the beets stay moist.

Peel the beets using a clean towel while still warm so that the skin removes evenly. Chill completely. Cut into bite size pieces.

Directions for the Hibiscus Vinaigrette:
Toast ingredients for the spice sachet in a dry sauté pan: the whole black peppercorns, juniper berries and bay leaves. Put into a sachet.

Place the spice sachet in a pot with the hibiscus, 2 1/2 cups vinegar, sugar, 1 cup water, 1 split vanilla bean, and 1 tablespoon salt and bring to a boil. Turn off the heat and steep for 45 minutes. Allow to completely cool. Remove sachet. In a Vita-Prep, food processer or blender blend until velvety smooth. Once smooth, add olive oil in a steady stream to emulsify.

Directions for Roasted Beet Salad Assembly:
Toss the roasted beets with a pinch of salt, pepper and enough vinaigrette to coat them evenly. Place onto a platter. Place the burrata across the beets. Garnish with strawberry slices. Sprinkle pistachios around evenly. Lightly dress the greens with hibiscus vinaigrette and a pinch of salt and pepper. Arrange loosely on top of the beets and enjoy!

Photo by Linda Blue

Tempeh Salad

Recipe Courtesy Chef Odin Macias

Servings: 8
Prep Time: 25 minutes

Ingredients for the Tempeh Salad:
1 pound tempeh
2 tablespoons extra virgin olive
7 ounces cucumber, diced
4 ounces red bell pepper, diced
1 ounce organic baby spinach
1 ounce watercress
1/2 ounce dandelion greens
1/2 teaspoon garlic
1 tablespoon ginger, chopped
1/4 cup rice vinegar
1 tablespoon yellow [Shiro] miso
1/4 teaspoon black pepper
1/4 cup sesame oil

Directions for the Tempeh Salad:
Preheat oven to 350° F.

Cut tempeh into small cubes. Place on a baking sheet and add 2 tablespoons olive oil to coat. Toast for 12 minutes. Place in the refrigerator to cool.

Mix together the cucumber, red bell pepper, spinach, watercress and dandelion greens.

Directions for the Dressing:
In a blender, mix the garlic, ginger, rice vinegar, miso and black pepper.

Slowly add sesame oil until well mixed.

Combine the toasted tempeh, vegetables, dressing and serve.

LAZY ACRES MARKET

302 Meigs Road
Santa Barbara, CA 93109
www.lazyacres.com

805.564.4410

Santa Barbara Culinary Arts | page 72

LOS ARROYOS
La Gringa
Recipe Courtesy Chef Tony Arroyo

Servings: 4
Prep Time: 20 minutes

Ingredients for La Gringa:
1/2 pound pork loin
salt and pepper
4 ounces achiote (Mexican annatto spice)
6 ounces orange juice
12 ounces fresh pineapple
1 jumbo red onion
1 ounce vegetable oil
8 6-inch flour tortillas
1/4 pound Jack cheese
1/4 pound Mozzarella cheese
salsa

Directions for La Gringa:
Tenderize pork loin and cut into thin slices. Lightly grill or pan sear the slices and season with salt and pepper. Then cut into 1" cubes.

Dissolve the achiote with the 6 ounces of orange juice and mix until creamy. Cut the pineapple into cubes. Julienne the red onion.

Put all the ingredients into a bowl or zip-close bag and marinate for at least one hour. Add the oil to a large frying pan over medium high heat. Slowly pour in the marinated pork, pineapple and onion and cook until the meat is crispy and red in color. Cover the pan and remove from heat to let the meat cook from the heat of the pan for 10-12 minutes, then remove to a plate to cool.

In a new frying pan, heat 2 tortillas at a time. Mix both cheeses together in a bowl, then put 1/8 of the cheese mixture onto each tortilla. When the cheese has melted, add 1/8 of the cooked meat to each tortilla and fold each in half. Repeat for the remaining tortillas.

On each plate, place two of the gringas crisscrossing each other. Add a dollop of salsa.

LOS ARROYOS

14 W. Figueroa Street
Santa Barbara, CA 93101
www.losarroyos.net

805.965.5541

Photo by Linda Blue

LOS OLIVOS CAFE' & WINE MERCHANT
Fried Goat Cheese Stuffed Squash Blossoms with Romesco Sauce

Recipe Courtesy Chef Chris Joslyn

Servings: 4
Prep Time: 1 hour 10 minutes

Ingredients for the Fried Goat Cheese Stuffed Blossoms:
1/2 small shallot, minced
1 cup goat cheese
1/4 cup olive oil
1/8 cup sherry or red wine vinegar
salt and pepper
16 squash blossoms
3 Roma tomatoes
1 large red bell pepper
1 small ancho chile
canola oil
1/4 cup hazelnuts
1/4 cup almonds
2 slices day old French bread, crust removed, diced
1 clove garlic, minced
1/2 teaspoon red pepper flakes
1/4 cup red wine vinegar
1 cup AP flour
1 tablespoon cornstarch
1 1/2 cups seltzer water

LOS OLIVOS CAFE' & WINE MERCHANT

2879 Grand Avenue
Los Olivos, CA 93441
www.losolivoscafe.com

333-WINES4U (888-946-3748)

Directions for the Fried Goat Cheese Stuffed Blossoms:
Combine the shallot, goat cheese, olive oil and sherry. Season to taste with salt and pepper. Place into a piping bag. Stuff the blossoms with the goat cheese mixture up to the point where the flower petals begin to split. Close up each blossom around the cheese.

Directions for the Romesco Sauce:
Put the oven rack in the middle position and preheat the oven to 400°F. Line a small baking pan with foil.

Roast the tomatoes and pepper in the pan until tender and browned, about 45 minutes. While the tomato is roasting, slit open the chile lengthwise, discard the stem and seeds, then tear it into small pieces.

Heat a small amount of oil in an 8- to 10-inch heavy skillet over moderate heat until hot but not smoking, then add the chile and cook, stirring, until fragrant and brighter red, 30 seconds to 1 minute. Transfer chile with a slotted spoon to a heatproof bowl.

Add the hazelnuts to the skillet along with almonds, bread, garlic and red pepper flakes and cook, stirring, until bread and garlic are golden, 2 to 3 minutes. Add to the chile in the bowl and let cool slightly.

Transfer to a food processor. Add bread and chile mixture, vinegar, and 1/4 teaspoon salt and purée until smooth. Thin with water if desired and adjust seasonings to taste.

Directions for the Tempura Batter:
Mix the flour, cornstarch and seltzer water until smooth.

Heat approximately 3 inches of canola oil in a medium-sized pot to 350°F. If you do not have a thermometer, drop some batter in the oil. If it floats immediately, it is ready. Working in batches of 3 or 4, dip the blossoms in the tempura and drop immediately in the oil. Use a slotted spoon to push them around the oil. Cook until golden, about 20-30 seconds. Remove with slotted spoon and place on a paper towel to remove excess oil. Serve with room-temperature Romesco sauce.

LOUISE'S KITCHEN TABLE
Berry Swirl Cheesecake
Recipe Courtesy Chef Louise Smith

Servings: 12-16
Prep Time: 1 1/2 hours plus chilling

Ingredients for the Berry Swirl Cheesecake:
butter for greasing
1 cup graham crackers, finely ground (about 8 sheets)
2 tablespoons unsalted butter, melted
1 1/4 cups sugar, in three parts
6 ounces raspberries (about 1.5 cups)
4 packages of 8-ounce cream cheese, room temperature
pinch of salt
1 teaspoon vanilla extract
4 eggs, at room temperature

Direction for the Berry Swirl Cheesecake:
Preheat the oven to 350° F. Grease a 9-inch spring form pan.

Stir together the graham cracker crumbs with the melted butter and 2 tablespoons of the sugar in a small bowl. Press crumb mixture onto the bottom of the pan.

Bake until set, about 10 minutes. Let cool in the pan on a wire rack. Reduce oven temperature to 325° F.

Process raspberries in a food processor until smooth, about 30 seconds. Pass the puree through a fine sieve into a small bowl and discard the solids. Whisk in 2 tablespoons of the sugar and set aside.

Cream the cream cheese in an electric mixer with the paddle attachment. Mix on medium for about 3 minutes until smooth. Scrape down the sides of the bowl and mix on low, adding the rest of the sugar in a slow stream. Add the salt and vanilla and mix until well combined. Add the eggs, one at a time, mixing each until just combined (do not over mix). Pour over the cooled crust.

Drop the raspberry sauce by the teaspoonful on top. With a toothpick or wooden skewer, swirl sauce into the cream cheese filling.

Place pan on a cookie sheet or in a roasting pan and bake until set, but remaining slightly wobbly in the center, about 60 minutes.

Transfer cake to a wire rack and let cool. Refrigerate for at least 8 hours, preferably overnight.

LOUISE'S KITCHEN TABLE

P.O. Box 45
Solvang, CA 93464
www.louiseskitchentable.com

805.403.9649

Photo by Linda Blue

L'S KITCHEN
LORRAINE LIM CATERING
Golden Bar Potstickers
with Tropical Salsa

Recipe Courtesy Owners Lorraine Lim
and Glenn Fout

Servings: 6 for a main course with salad or 10 for appetizers
Prep Time: 1 hour

Ingredients for the Golden Bar Potstickers and Tropical Salsa:
1/2 lb of each: ground chicken, ground pork, ground shrimp
    Note: Use any combination!
2 scallions/green onions, chopped
1/4 cup cilantro, chopped, plus extra for garnish
3 tablespoons cornstarch
2 tablespoons + 1/4 cup sesame oil, in two parts
2 teaspoons white pepper
3 tablespoons garlic, chopped
2 tablespoons ginger, chopped
2 tablespoons sherry
2 tablespoons + 1/4 cup soy sauce, in two parts
salt to taste
wonton skins, square
vegetable oil to fry potstickers
1/4 cup of water or chicken stock
(continued at right)

L'S KITCHEN - LORRAINE LIM CATERING

121 East Yanonali Street
Santa Barbara, CA 93101
www.lorrainelimcatering.com

805.962.7550

Ingredients (continued from left):
1 ripe banana
1/4 cup rice vinegar
1/4 cup sesame oil
orange zest and 1/4 cup orange juice
chile flakes to taste or a squeeze of sriracha hot sauce
cilantro sprigs for garnish

Directions for the Golden Bar Potstickers:
In a large bowl, mix the ground meat together with the scallions, cilantro, cornstarch, 2 tablespoons sesame oil, white pepper, garlic, ginger, sherry, 2 tablespoons soy sauce and salt.

On a dry clean surface, lay out your wonton skins 10 at a time. Using a spoon, place about a tablespoon of meat filling on one end of each wonton skin and roll up like a cigar or burrito. Place on a parchment-covered sheet pan, being sure to leave a bit of space between each potsticker so they don't stick together. Repeat until all skins are filled.

Heat a non-stick fry pan over medium heat, then add a bit of vegetable oil (1 tablespoon). Fry the bottom of the potstickers, a few at a time, making sure you don't crowd your pan and there is space between potstickers, until golden brown, turning with tongs. When browned, add 1/4 cup of water or chicken stock, cover, turn the heat down and let steam until done, about 2 or 3 minutes. Finish cooking the remaining potstickers in batches until all potstickers are cooked.

Directions for the Tropical Salsa:
Place the banana, 1/4 cup soy sauce, rice vinegar, 1/4 cup sesame oil, zest and orange juice into blender, blend until smooth. Season to taste with chili flakes or sriracha.

Serve potstickers warm with tropical salsa, garnished with cilantro sprigs.

Photo by Linda Blue

MICHAEL'S CATERING
Soufflé Suissesse V.O.
Recipe Courtesy Chef Michael Hutchings

Servings: 8
Prep Time: 40 minutes

Ingredients for the Soufflé Suissesse V.O.:
1/4 cup butter, plus extra for buttering molds
1/2 cup flour
3 cups milk
salt and ground white pepper
3 egg yolks
8 ounces Gruyère cheese, grated, in two parts
4 cups heavy cream
6 egg whites

MICHAEL'S CATERING

22 W. Mission Street Suite G
Santa Barbara, CA 93101
www.michaelscateringSB.com

805.568.1896

Directions for the Soufflé Suissesse V.O.:
Chill eight 4-inch round by 1-inch high soufflé molds in the freezer while preparing béchamel sauce. Butter the chilled soufflé molds and set aside.

Preheat oven to 425° F.

Directions for the Béchamel Sauce:
In a medium saucepan, bring milk to a boil, then set aside. In a large heavy-bottomed skillet or sauté pan, melt the 1/4 cup butter over low heat. Stir in the flour and cook 3 minutes, whisking constantly to prevent coloring. Allow to cool slightly.

Whisk the hot milk into the butter/flour mixture. Bring to a boil over medium heat and season to taste with salt and white pepper.

Reduce heat and simmer 3 minutes, whisking constantly to avoid lumps. Remove from heat and whisk in the egg yolks, one by one, mixing well after each addition. Stir in 3 ounces of the grated cheese. Transfer mixture to a large bowl, then set aside. Cover to keep hot.

Directions for the Cream Sauce:
In a large heavy-bottomed skillet, heat the cream until warm; do not allow to boil. Salt to taste. Set aside and keep warm.

Directions for the Soufflé:
Beat egg whites with whisk or electric mixer until stiff peaks form. Whisk one-third of egg whites into the bowl of prepared béchamel sauce. Gently fold in the remainder of egg whites with a spatula (must be perfectly blended to ensure a smooth consistency but do not over mix).

Fill each prepared mold until slightly mounded. Place filled molds on a baking sheet and bake 5 minutes or until tops are slightly browned and the mixture has risen.

Place a pool of cream into an oven proof ceramic single-serving dish. Gently turn each soufflé out into the prepared serving dish. Sprinkle generously with grated cheese and return to oven for an additional 5-6 minutes until the cheese has melted and is slightly browned.

Serve immediately on an underliner plate with a spoon.

MONTECITO COUNTRY CLUB
Wild Mushroom Strudel
with Corn Coulis

Recipe Courtesy Executive Chef Michael Blackwell

Servings: 6
Prep Time: 1 hour

Ingredients for the Wild Mushroom Strudel:
1 shallot, finely diced + 1 shallot, roughly chopped
9 tablespoons butter (no need to be melted), in two parts
1 cup shiitake mushrooms, julienned
1 cup oyster mushrooms, torn into strips
Kosher salt and fresh ground pepper
3 cloves garlic, minced, in two parts
1 16-ounce box frozen phyllo dough sheets, thawed in the
   refrigerator
9 tablespoons butter, melted
6 ounces goat cheese
1 tablespoon fresh thyme, minced
3 ears fresh corn, cut off the cob
1/2 cup heavy cream
micro greens
olive oil

MONTECITO COUNTRY CLUB

920 Summit Road
Santa Barbara, CA 93108
www.montecitocc.com

805.969.3216

Directions for the Wild Mushroom Strudel:
Preheat the oven to 350° F.

Sweat the finely diced shallot in 3 tablespoons butter over medium heat in a sauté pan until translucent but not browned. Add the mushrooms and a pinch of salt and pepper and sauté until lightly browned. Add 2 cloves of the minced garlic and sauté for another two minutes. Remove from the pan and cool to room temperature.

Unroll thawed but cold phyllo and peel away one layer. Place it on a kitchen towel or plastic wrap on a flat surface and brush with melted butter across the entire surface. Repeat until you have 5 layers of phyllo. Place one sixth of the mushroom filling and one ounce of the goat cheese in the center of the narrower edge of the phyllo, leaving two inches from the edge and sides. Wrap the phyllo around the mushroom and cheese mix like you are folding a burrito. Fold over the top, fold in the sides and roll to the end. Be sure to wrap it tight so that it will hold its shape. Place the strudel on a baking sheet tray and repeat these steps until you have six strudels. Each strudel should be four inches long and one inch in diameter. Brush the strudels with melted butter and bake for 15-20 minutes or until golden brown.

Directions for the Corn Coulis:
Cook the chopped shallot, 1 clove of minced garlic and thyme in 1 tablespoon butter over medium heat in a sauté pan until translucent Add the corn and sauté for five minutes or until golden brown. Add the cream and cook for another five minutes, stirring regularly, until the cream is reduced by half. Pour the mixture into a blender, secure the lid with a kitchen towel and blend until smooth. Finish with a pinch of salt and white pepper to taste.

Directions for Assembling the Dish:
Ladle one ounce of the warm corn coulis onto a plate and swirl into a circle the size of a tennis ball. Cut the strudel in half at an angle and place on the plate so that one half rests on the other for height. Garnish with a pinch of micro greens and drizzle with olive oil.

Note: Use the freshest frozen phyllo dough. Don't use dough that has sat too long in the freezer.

MONTECITO WINE BISTRO
Ahi Sushi Bites
Recipe Courtesy Chef Victor Carranza

Servings: 8 (six pieces each)
Prep Time: 2 hours

Ingredients for the Ahi Sushi Bites:
1 cup white rice, cooked
1 cup brown rice, cooked
2 ounces balsamic reduction
2 ounces + 1/2 cup soy sauce, in two parts
1 teaspoon corn starch
2 cups tempura batter
oil for deep-frying
2 tablespoons olive oil
1 pound of #1 sushi-grade ahi steaks
salt and pepper
1/2 cup orange juice
1 teaspoon ginger
1/2 cup brown sugar
1 cup mayonnaise
1/3 cup sriracha hot sauce
3 lemons, juiced
wasabi caviar for garnish
daikon sprouts for garnish

Directions for the Rice Cakes:
Combine the white and brown rice, the balsalmic reduction, 2 ounces soy sauce and corn starch. Form eight small cakes and place in the freezer for at least 45 minutes.

Mix the tempura batter just before frying. (Making it ahead will produce a heavy coating.) Be sure the water used is very cold to make a cold batter that will remain light when fried. Dip each cake in the tempura batter and then fry the patties over high heat in oil (use a deep fryer for better results) for about 4 minutes on each side. Be sure the oil is the proper temperature. If it's not hot enough, the batter will absorb oil and the result will be greasy tempura.

Directions for Ahi:
Place a skillet over medium-high heat and coat with 2 tablespoons of olive oil. Season the tuna generously with salt and pepper. Lay the tuna in the hot oil and sear for 1 minute on each side to form a slight crust.

Directions for the Ponzu Sauce:
Mix together 1/2 cup soy sauce, orange juice, ginger and brown sugar.

Directions for the Sriracha Aioli:
Mix together the mayonnaise, sriracha, lemon juice, 1 teaspoon salt and 1 teaspoon pepper.

Directions for Assembling the Dish:
Spread the Sriracha aioli over each cake then the Ponzu sauce. Cut each cake into 6 pieces. Slice the ahi into 48 pieces. Place one slice of seared ahi over each piece of the cake and garnish with wasabi caviar and daikon sprouts. Enjoy it!

MONTECITO WINE BISTRO

516 San Ysidro Road
Montecito, CA 93108
www.pierrelafond.com

805.969.7520

Photo by Linda Blue

NEW WEST CATERING
INDUSTRIAL EATS
White Shrimp, Pancetta, Chilies and Garlic

Recipe Courtesy Chef Jeff Olsson

Servings: 4
Prep Time: 20 minutes

Ingredients for White Shrimp, Pancetta, Chilies and Garlic:
12 Mexican white shrimp, peeled and deveined
12 slices pancetta
1 ounce olive oil
2 cloves garlic, sliced thinly
1 Fresno chile, sliced thinly
4 ounces good-quality white wine
4 ounces cold butter, cubed
juice of 1 lemon
salt and pepper
1 ounce parsley, chopped
crusty bread, toasted

Directions for White Shrimp, Pancetta, Chilies and Garlic:
Wrap each shrimp with one strip of the pancetta. Heat the olive oil in a 10" iron skillet until the oil just begins to smoke. Carefully add the shrimp to the pan. Cook 3 to 4 minutes per side, then remove and keep warm.

Add the garlic and chile, stirring to cover in olive oil/pancetta fat. Deglaze with wine, then reduce by half.

Add the cold, cubed butter and swirl pan to incorporate and emulsify the butter and wine together.

Season with lemon, salt and pepper to taste. Add the chopped parsley.

Serve the shrimp and sauce over toasted crusty bread.

INDUSTRIAL EATS

181 Industrial Way
Buellton, CA 93427
www.newwestcatering.com • www.industrialeats.com
jeff@newwestcatering.com

805.688.0991

Photo by Linda Blue

NIMITA'S CUISINE
Vegetable Korma Curry
Recipe Courtesy Chef Nimita Dhirajlal
Servings: 6
Prep Time: 1 hour

Ingredients for the Vegetable Korma Curry:
2 tablespoons ghee
1 teaspoon curry powder
1 tablespoon garam masala
1/2 ground cumin
1/2 teaspoon ground nutmeg
1/2 teaspoon cinnamon
1 onion, sliced in wedges
4 cloves garlic, minced
1 (16 ounce) can chopped tomatoes with juice
1 (4 ounce) can chopped mild chile with juice
2 cups vegetable broth
2 medium Yukon potatoes, peeled and cubed
3 cups cauliflower florets
2 carrots, peeled, halved and sliced
2 cups fresh green beans, cut into 1 inch pieces
1 tablespoon fresh cilantro, chopped
1 red or orange pepper, seeds removed and sliced
1 (16 ounce) can unsweetened coconut milk
1 teaspoon cashew nut butter or 1/2 cup of ground unsalted
    cashews
1 cup plain yogurt (eliminate if on a vegan diet)
1 tablespoon cashews, chopped for garnish
salt to taste

NIMITA'S CUISINE

3765 Torino Drive
Santa Barbara, CA 93101
www.nimitascuisine.com

805.259.6594

Directions for the Vegetable Korma Curry:
Heat the ghee in a large frying pan or a medium-sized stainless steel pot over medium-low heat. Add the curry powder, garam masala, cumin, nutmeg and cinnamon and allow to cook, stirring occasionally, for 2 minutes. Be careful not to burn the spices!

Mix in the onion and garlic and cook until the onion is semi-cooked. Add the tomatoes and juice, green chile, green chile juice and vegetable broth and bring to a simmer.

Mix in the potatoes, cauliflower, carrots, green beans, and cilantro; cover and cook over medium-low heat for 25 to 30 minutes, until vegetables are tender but firm.

Mix in sliced pepper, coconut milk and cashew butter or ground cashews. Cook 15 minutes.

Remove from heat, stir in yogurt (optional) and season to taste with salt.

Serve over basmati rice and garnish with chopped cashews.

OLIO E LIMONE RISTORANTE
Santa Barbara Spot Prawns with Spicy Fresh Oregano Oil

Recipe Courtesy Chef and Proprietors
Alberto and Elaine Morello

Servings: 4
Prep Time: 30 minutes

Ingredients for the Santa Barbara Spot Prawns with Spicy Fresh
    Oregano Oil:
2 pounds Santa Barbara spot prawns
sea salt
freshly ground black pepper
1 cup extra-virgin olive oil, in two parts
4 fresh garlic cloves, sliced
2 teaspoons spicy oil (alternately, you can use 1 teaspoon dry
    crushed red pepper flakes in the oil)
1 bunch (approximately 1/2 cup) fresh oregano leaves plus 4 tips
    for garnish
2 Eureka lemons, halved

OLIO E LIMONE RISTORANTE
OLIO CRUDO BAR
OLIO PIZZERIA®

11 West Victoria Street, Suite 17, 18 and 21
Santa Barbara, CA 93101
www.oliocucina.com

805.899.2699

Directions for the Santa Barbara Spot Prawns with Spicy Fresh
    Oregano Oil:

Using a small knife or by hand, remove the shrimp shells leaving the head
and tail tip on.

Heat 1/2 cup olive oil in a small sauté pan over medium heat. Add garlic
and sauté until golden. Add the spicy oil (or chili flakes in olive oil) and
oregano leaves, stir, remove from heat and set aside.

In a medium sauté pan, add the remaining 1/2 cup of the olive oil. When
the oil reaches a high temperature, add the prawns. Cook them on one
side then the other briefly.

Arrange the shrimp on heated plates. Drizzle some of the spicy oil/
oregano mix over the prawns using a spoon.

Serve with lemon halves and garnish with fresh oregano tips.

Locations now open at The Shoppes Westlake Village.
www.oliocucina.com

Photo by Linda Blue

Photos by Kevin Steele

OPAL RESTAURANT AND BAR
"Like Water for Chocolate" Surprise

Recipe Courtesy Chef Felipe Barajas
Owners Tina Takaya and Richard Yates

Servings: 6-8 chocolate surprises depending on the size of mold
Prep Time: 1 hour

Ingredients for the Fresh Raspberry Coulis
2 cups fresh raspberries
1/2 cup to 3/4 cup sugar, to taste
38 ounces dark chocolate (Belgian Callebaut recommended),
    in two parts
10 egg whites, in two parts
2 pints heavy whipping cream, in two parts
6 ounces white chocolate (Belgian Callebaut recommended)
6-8 sprigs of mint as garnish (optional)

Note: The movie is a classic. Taken from the Magical Realism book, "Like Water for Chocolate" written by Laura Esquivel, the "Cinderella meets Romeo and Juliet story" takes place in Mexico and revolves around a gifted young woman's search for the fulfillment of her life's passions. Denied the opportunity to marry the love of her life, her magical gift expresses itself through her amazing culinary skill. When she cooks she puts all the emotions of her life into the food she prepares, hence everyone who tastes her food feels her emotions. This dessert was created with a similar passion. In 2010, we had a book signing event with Laura Esquivel, and offered the wedding menu from her book as well as the "Like Water for Chocolate" Surprise for dessert.

OPAL RESTAURANT AND BAR

1325 State Street
Santa Barbara, CA 93101
www.opalrestaurantandbar.com

805.966.9676

Directions for the Raspberry Coulis:
Set aside 6-8 raspberries for garnish. Put the rest of the raspberries, 1 cup water and 1/2 cup sugar into a pot and bring to a boil until thick. Add more sugar to taste. Cool down and put in the refrigerator.

Directions for the Dark Chocolate Mousse:
Melt 6 ounces dark chocolate in a double boiler. Transfer to a medium bowl to let cool to room temperature. Whip the egg whites in a bowl until stiff peaks form, then add 2/3 cup sugar and whip one more minute. Whip the heavy cream until stiff. Gently fold together the egg whites and cream. Reserve half the egg white/cream mixture for the White Chocolate Mousse.

To continue making the Dark Chocolate Mousse, fold in the melted dark chocolate into the first half of the egg white/cream mixture until fully integrated. Set aside.

Directions for the White Chocolate Mousse:
Melt 6 ounces white chocolate in a double boiler. Transfer to a medium bowl to let cool to room temperature. Take the remaining egg whites/cream mixture and fold in the melted white chocolate until fully integrated. Set aside.

Directions for the Dark Chocolate Shell:
Melt 32 ounces dark chocolate in a double boiler. Transfer to a medium bowl. Take a small dome mold, wrap in plastic wrap, twisting the plastic end under the dome. Holding the twisted part, dip the dome into the melted chocolate until it is covered, spin off the excess chocolate, then place the mold dome-side up on a wax-papered sheet pan. Put in the freezer until hard, approximately 5 minutes. Remove from the plastic immediately when out of the freezer.

Directions for Assembling the Dish:
Fill half of the chocolate dome with white chocolate mousse. Finish with the dark chocolate mousse.

Ladle a tablespoon of raspberry coulis on a plate and put a chocolate surprise (the dome of chocolate) in the middle. Garnish with a fresh raspberry (save some melted dark chocolate to secure the raspberry on top). Can use a small sprig of mint as well.

OSTERIA MONTE GRAPPA
Trenette Verdi al Pastore
with Mint Pesto

Recipe Courtesy Chef Stefano Bernardi

Servings: 6-8
Prep Time: 3 hours 30 minutes

Ingredients for the Trenette Verdi al Pastore with Mint Pesto:
1 leg of lamb, bone- in
2 cups carrots. diced
2 cups celery, diced
approximately 3 cups onion or leek, diced, in three parts
approximately 4 cups white wine, in two parts
4 tablespoons roasted garlic, in two parts
6 sprigs of fresh rosemary, plus approximately 1 teaspoon minced
6 sprigs of fresh thyme, plus approximately 1 teaspoon minced
4 bay leaves, dry
salt and pepper, to taste
approximately 4 cups of olive oil, in three parts
2 cups fresh mint with sprigs, washed
1/2 cup fresh parsley with sprigs, washed
1 tablespoon fresh lemon juice
1/2 cup pureed roasted garlic
6-8 servings of pasta, cooked al dente
feta cheese for garnish

OSTERIA MONTE GRAPPA

242 E. Ojai Avenue
Ojai, CA 93023
www.omgojai.com
omgojai@gmail.com
805.640.6767

Directions for the Roasted Lamb:
Preheat oven to 500° F.

Salt and pepper the lamb in a deep baking dish and place in the oven to brown for 15-20 minutes, checking frequently (we use an oak-burning oven). After browning evenly, remove the lamb and set aside. In the hot pan, spread the carrots, celery and 2 cups of the onion or leeks to sweat for 15-20 minutes.

Reduce oven temp to 400° F.

Place the lamb on top of the vegetables. Pour in 2 cups of wine then enough water to cover the vegetables. Put 3 tablespoons of garlic, 6 sprigs of rosemary, 6 sprigs of thyme and the bay leaves on top and cover pan with aluminum foil.

Cook for 2 1/2 hours or until the meat pulls away from the bone. Remove the lamb meat and set aside to let cool. Remove the herbs and bone and let the cooking liquid cool.

Directions for the Mint Pesto:
Put 3 cups of the olive oil, the mint, the parsley, 1 tablespoon roasted garlic, 1 tablespoon onion or leek and lemon juice in a blender. Puree on high until smooth. Adjust seasonings to taste.

Directions for Assembling the Dish:
Add 1 tablespoon olive oil to a hot pan over medium-high heat. Add 1 tablespoon of onion or leek and sweat for 30 seconds. Add 1 tablespoon roasted garlic puree and spread across the bottom of the pan. Stir in 4-6 ounces of shredded lamb meat then add 1/4 cup white wine and deglaze the pan—scraping up any browned bits into the sauce.

Add 1 1/2 cups of the cooking liquid and bring to a boil. Add a pinch of rosemary and a pinch of thyme. Cook until the sauce is reduced by half. When reduced enough to coat pasta without being soup-like, add al dente pasta and cook for 30-40 seconds. Adjust seasonings to taste.

Add 3 tablespoons of the Mint Pesto and fold together thoroughly to warm. Plate and top with feta cheese.

Photo by Linda Blue

PALACE GRILL
Louisiana Bread Pudding Soufflé
Recipe Courtesy General Manager Errol Williams

Servings: 8
Prep Time: 1 hour 15 minutes

Ingredients for the Louisiana Bread Pudding Soufflé:
approximately 2 1/2 cups sugar, in three parts
1 quart of half-and-half or whipping cream
1/4 cup corn starch
1/2 cup bourbon whiskey
2 tablespoons + 1/4 teaspoon vanilla extract, in two parts
2 tablespoons raisins
1 1/2 teaspoons cinnamon
3 whole eggs + 4 egg whites, in two parts
2 teaspoons Grand Marnier
3/4 cup flour
6 tablespoons water
1/4 cup butter plus extra for greasing
powdered sugar

Directions for the Bourbon Cream Sauce:
Bring 1 1/2 cups sugar and the half-and-half to a boil. Dissolve the cornstarch in the bourbon and 2 tablespoons vanilla, then add to sauce. Cook, stirring, until sauce thickens.

Directions for Soufflé:
Preheat oven to 325° F.

Combine raisins and cinnamon. Set aside.

Lightly beat the whole eggs, Grand Marnier and 1/4 teaspoon vanilla in a separate bowl.

Place flour and 1/4 cup granulated sugar in electric mixer bowl. Bring water and butter to boil in a saucepan, then add to flour mixture while mixer is on medium speed.

Reduce speed of the mixer and add the egg mixture slowly but continuously to flour mixture, beating about 4 minutes. Set aside.

In a clean, dry mixer bowl, beat the egg whites and 1/2 cup of granulated sugar at high speed until stiff peaks form. Lightly but thoroughly fold the egg white mixture into the soufflé batter. Fold in the raisin-cinnamon mixture.

Butter 8 individual (3 inch) soufflé cups and sprinkle with granulated sugar. Fill each about ¾ full of batter. Bake until golden brown and puffy, about 25 minutes. Dust immediately with powdered sugar.

Serve with the warm Bourbon Cream Sauce to pour on the soufflés at the table.

PALACE GRILL

8 East Cota Street
Santa Barbara, CA 93101
www.palacegrill.com

805.963.5000

PALACE GRILL
Louisiana Bread Pudding Soufflé

Photo by Linda Blue

Santa Barbara Culinary Arts | page 101

REFUGIO RANCH
Acorn Squash Stuffed with Cumin-Hazelnut-Quinoa and Gruyère

Recipe Courtesy Food Editor Tama Takahashi
Servings: 4
Prep Time: 1 hour

Ingredients for the Acorn Squash Stuffed with Cumin-Hazelnut-Quinoa and Gruyère:
2 small acorn squash
2 tablespoons butter, melted
2 cups chicken or vegetable stock
1 cup quinoa
1 bay leaf
2 tablespoons extra virgin olive oil
1/4 small onion, small dice
1 clove garlic, minced
1/8 teaspoon cinnamon
2 teaspoons ground cumin
1 teaspoon paprika
1/2 teaspoon turmeric
1/4 cup red or orange bell pepper, small dice
1/2 teaspoon sea salt
freshly ground black pepper
1/2 cup dried Montmorency cherries
1/2 cup soft-dried Turkish apricots, sliced thinly
1/2 cup hazelnuts, freshly toasted
1/2 cup grated Gruyère cheese

REFUGIO RANCH

2990 Grand Avenue
Los Olivos, CA 93441
www.refugioranch.com

805.688.5400

Directions for the Acorn Squash Stuffed with Cumin-Hazelnut-Quinoa and Gruyère:

Preheat the oven to 350 ° F.

Cut the squash in half, scoop out the seeds (an apple corer works well) and pat the squash dry with paper towels. Brush the inside with butter. Put on a lined baking sheet and roast for 50 minutes.

In the meantime, cook the quinoa in stock and bay leaf in a saucepan by bringing to a boil, then simmering until the liquid is almost absorbed. Turn off the heat, cover and let sit. Remove the bay leaf.

Sweat the onion and garlic in oil, then add the cinnamon, cumin, paprika, turmeric and bell pepper. Stir and cook for 2 minutes. Then add to the quinoa along with salt and black pepper to taste. Stir in the cherries, apricots and hazelnuts.

Note: if you have leftover quinoa—save it to make a quick and delicious soup with chicken stock and spinach.

Remove the squash halves from the oven and stuff with quinoa mixture. Top with grated Gruyère and return to the oven to bake until the cheese is melted and golden brown, about 10 minutes.

Created for the Refugio Ranch Ineseño.

Our Ineseño (the name refers to the indigenous peoples of Santa Ynez) is comprised of 59% Roussane and 41% Viognier. Packed with depth and concentration, this is certainly the richest white in the Refugio Ranch lineup. Loaded with layers of marmalade, citrus oil, poached pear, jasmine, and wild herbs. The wine balances the honeyed nuttiness and viscosity of Roussanne with the more floral, ginger, peach, and tropical elements of Viognier. Not shy by any means, offering decadence, yet poised with balanced acidity keeping it fresh.

91 points - Beverage Tasting Institute

Photo by Linda Blue

RENAUD'S PATISSERIE
The Strawberry Rhubarb Tartlette
Recipe Courtesy Chef Thomas Comte

Servings: 4
Prep Time: 2 hours

Rhubarb Chip Ingredients:
1 stalk fresh rhubarb
1 cup water
1 cup sugar

Shortbread Ingredients:
1 1/2 cup butter
5-6 hard-boiled egg yolks
1 cup powdered sugar
9/10 teaspoon "Fleur de Sel" salt
      (*nine tenths of a teaspoon)
2 4/5 cups all-purpose flour
2.3 ounces potato starch

Rhubarb Compote Ingredients:
35 ounces fresh rhubarb, sliced
1 cup sugar
1 lemon, juiced
3 1/2 ounces pomegranate juice

Chantilly Ingredients:
3 1/2 ounces cold mascarpone
8 ounces cold whipping cream
1 ounce sugar
1 vanilla bean or 1/4 teaspoon
      vanilla extract

Additional Ingredients:
12 strawberries, halved
white chocolate ring
      (optional)

RENAUD'S PATISSERIE

3315 State Street
Santa Barbara, CA 93105
www.renaudsbakery.com
info@renaudsbakery.com
805.569.2400

Directions for the Rhubarb Chips:
Preheat the oven to 190°F.

Begin with the rhubarb chips - they will need to be soaked in a syrup before drying in the oven. To make the syrup, bring 1 cup water and 1 cup sugar to a boil. Remove from heat and let sit for 30 minutes to cool. Using an apple peeler, peel the stick of rhubarb length-wise to create long, thin peelings. Soak the rhubarb peelings in the syrup for 30 minutes minimum. Place the peelings flat onto a silpat mat and dry them in the oven for one hour or more to "crystallize". Remove from oven and shape the chips in a ring while they are still warm. This will serve as the decor.

Directions for the Shortbread:
Adjust the oven temperature to 300°F.

Use a paddle to cream butter in a stand mixer. Press the hard-boiled yolks through a fine sifter to obtain 25 grams of powder and add to the butter. Slowly add the powdered sugar, salt, flour and potato starch. Be careful not to overwork the dough. Place the dough in the refrigerator until firm, about 30 minutes minimum. (Note: Best to do this the day before.) Once firm, roll out the dough and use a 3-4" diameter circle cutter to cut discs. Bake discs for 15-20 minutes.

Directions for the Rhubarb Compote:
Stew the diced rhubarb, sugar, lemon and pomegranate juices in a pot for 15-20 minutes on low heat. Strain and reserve.

Directions for the Mascarpone Chantilly:
The Chantilly ingredients should be very cold and fresh to be whipped. Soften the mascarpone with a whisk or spoon (do not heat). Add the cream, sugar and vanilla. Whip until firm.

Directions for Assembling the Tartlette:
Top shortbread disc with rhubarb compote. Place a white chocolate ring on the compote (optional). Arrange 6 strawberry halves in a circle. Place the rhubarb chip decor and spoon a dollop of the Chantilly in the center.

SANTA BARBARA TAMALES-TO-GO
Tomatillo Salsa
Recipe Courtesy Chef Richard Lambert

Servings: two quarts
Prep Time: 1 hour

Ingredients for the Tomatillo Salsa:
2 white onions, quartered
5 cloves garlic, unpeeled
3 serrano chiles
3 pounds (22-25) tomatillos, outer skins removed, washed
5 poblano chiles
3 teaspoons cumin seed
2 teaspoons Mexican oregano
2 teaspoons coriander seed
2 tablespoons vegetable oil
1 cup or more chicken broth or water
salt to taste
cilantro optional

SANTA BARBARA TAMALES-TO-GO

1139 Alameda Padre Serra
Santa Barbara, CA 93103
www.sbtamalestogo.com

805.965.2321

Directions for the Tomatillo Salsa:
Fire roast the onions, garlic and serrano chiles on a comal or cast-iron skillet over the burner for 10-15 minutes, turning several times to char all sides. Fire roast the tomatillos and the poblano chiles under the broiler, turning to char all sides.

Place poblanos in a plastic bag for 15 minutes to steam from their own heat, then peel away the outer skin and remove the seeds, stem and placenta [membrane]. Do not wash the poblanos because that will diminish their natural flavor.

Peel the roasted garlic and place all the fire-roasted ingredients in a blender for 20-30 seconds, then set aside.

Toast the cumin and coriander seeds for several minutes in a sauté pan. Put in a spice grinder with the oregano and blend for 8-10 seconds.

Heat the oil in a large skillet, add the spice mixture and fry for 2-3 minutes. Add the ingredients from the blender. Note: The blended ingredients will "spit" when poured into the hot oil, so be cautious and pour slowly. After a minute, lower the heat to medium and simmer for 5 minutes. Add the chicken broth or water while cooking to thin the salsa to desired consistency. Keep in mind the salsa will thicken a little naturally after it cools. Add salt to taste. You may refrigerate this salsa up to five days or freeze for several months

Note: Cilantro is often used in tomatillo salsa recipes. If you like the flavor, add up to one cup of cilantro leaves to the fire-roasted ingredients before blending.

This salsa is a favorite among my customers. Tomatillos have a note of citrus flavor which creates a perfect counterpoint to the chile and spices in the recipe. We use the salsa to make both our chicken and vegetable tamales. It is also delicious with enchiladas as well as chilaquiles.

SANTA BARBARA WINERY
Shrimp Bites with Wasabi-Yuzu Aioli
Recipe Courtesy Food Editor Tama Takahashi

Servings: 2
Prep time: 15 minutes

Ingredients for the Asian-Inspired Shrimp Bites:
1/2 cup mayonnaise
1 teaspoon yuzu (Japanese citrus juice)
1/2 teaspoon dry wasabi powder
salt
approximately 12 Chinese pea pods
4 jumbo shrimp
flour
3 egg yolks
1 teaspoon sugar
1/2 teaspoon mirin (Japanese cooking sake)
1 teaspoon usukuchi soy sauce (light soy sauce)
1 tablespoon melted unsalted butter, at room temperature
2 teaspoons chives, minced
2 teaspoons fresh ginger, minced

Directions for the Wasabi-Yuzu Aioli:
Mix the mayonnaise, yuzu and wasabi powder. Season to taste with salt. Thin with just enough water so the sauce will flow from a squeeze bottle. Put into the squeeze bottle and set aside.

Directions for the Shrimp Bites:
Bring a small pot of water and big pinch of salt to a boil. Cook the pea pods just until they turn bright green, then transfer to an ice bath, approximately 1 minute. When they are cool, drain on paper towels.

Peel the shrimp, salt liberally and let sit 1 minute. Wash with cold water and pat dry with paper towels. Cut lengthwise in half, removing the vein.

Using a sharp knife, cut shallow cuts in a grid pattern on the cut side of each shrimp. This will keep the shrimp from curling when they cook. Dredge in flour.

Mix the egg yolks, sugar, mirin, soy sauce, melted butter, chives and ginger.

Heat a non-stick or cast iron skillet over medium heat. Do not butter or oil. Dip the floured shrimp into the egg mixture and place on the skillet cut side down. Cook until the inside is golden brown, approximately 1 minute. Flip and cook the other side until light brown, approximately 1/2 to 1 minute, then remove to a side plate.

Plate the pea pods topped with the shrimp bites, then drizzle the wasabi-yuzu aioli on top.

Created for the Santa Barbara Winery 2013 Thompson Vineyard Pinot Gris, Santa Barbara County.

Winemaker's note: Picked ripe and then whole cluster pressed (including stems) to minimize phenolic extraction. A cool stainless steel fermentations maintains the crisp acidity of the wine while putting forth fresh apple and pear flavors.

SANTA BARBARA WINERY

202 Anacapa Street
Santa Barbara, CA 93101
www.sbwinery.com

805.963.3633

Photo by Tama Takahashi

SANTA BARBARA YACHT CLUB
Foie Gras Panna Cotta: Cardamom Peach Gelee, Elderflower Reduction, Toasted Sicilian Pistachio, Grilled Peach, and Brioche Toast Points

Recipe Courtesy Chef Mossin Sugich

Servings: 4
Prep Time: 1 hour 30 minutes, plus overnight pickling

Ingredients for the Foie Gras Panna Cotta: Cardamom Peach Gelee:
480 grams foie gras (optional: add 200 grams for hot preparation)
108 grams heavy cream
148 grams milk
50 grams + 150 grams elderflower liquor, in two parts
1 teaspoon + 1/4 teaspoon sea salt, in two parts
1/2 teaspoon ground black pepper
5 grams + 6 grams gelatin sheet, in two parts
1 small shallot, small dice
1 teaspoon + 1 teaspoon olive oil, in two parts, plus extra for
    peaches
2 ripe peaches + 2 peaches, each sliced into 6 pieces, in two parts
130 grams peach puree
1/2 lemon, zested and juiced
1/4 teaspoon sea salt
1/2 teaspoon + 1/2 teaspoon ground cardamom
3 tablespoons pistachios (Sicilian recommended)
1 brioche, sliced

SANTA BARBARA YACHT CLUB

130 Harbor Way
Santa Barbara, CA 93109
www.sbyc.com
mossin@sbyc.com
805.965.8112

Directions for the Foie Gras Panna Cotta:
In a cool area of the kitchen, lay the foie gras on its outside and follow the veins, removing carefully with the back of a paring knife. After cleaning, place in freezer for 5-10 minutes. Add cream, milk, 50 grams elderflower liquor, 1 teaspoon salt and 1/2 teaspoon pepper in a heavy-bottomed pan. Bring to a slight boil, then add the foie gras. Cook until the foie gras is halfway melted and semi-incorporated into the liquid. Remove from heat let sit for five minutes. While it cools, bloom 5 grams of gelatin in ice water for 5 minutes or until soft. Do the same separately with the 6 grams and set aside for the Peach Gelee.

Add the gelatin and warm foie gras mixture to a blender. Blend until smooth and emulsified. Strain through a fine strainer. Portion into ramekins then chill in the refrigerator for 2-3 hours.

Directions for the Peach Gelee:
In a heavy-bottomed stainless steel pot, sweat the shallot in 1 teaspoon olive oil until translucent. Add 2 peaches with their skins on to add some tartness. (Note: farmers market peaches recommended to avoid adding sugar—as they are naturally sweet.) Cook for five minutes then add peach puree, 150 grams elderflower liquor, lemon zest and juice, salt and 1/2 teaspoon cardamom. Cook until the ingredients are incorporated together then add bloomed 6 grams gelatin. Cool in the refrigerator until set to the desired consistency—either spoon-able or completely set to be cut into shapes.

Directions for the Pistachios:
Preheat the oven to 300° F. Lightly coat the pistachios in 1 teaspoon olive oil and 1/4 teaspoon sea salt, then roast in oven for 4 minutes. Slightly bring out oils and aroma. Note: Sicilian pistachios might be hard to get your hands on but they are worth the try, regular are just fine.

Directions for the Grilled Peach:
Lightly coat the slices of the remaining 2 peaches with oil, sprinkle with 1/2 teaspoon ground cardamom, then grill. (Note: Slightly firmer peaches will not melt away on the grill.) Toast the brioche until golden brown.

Note: Have a glass of wine or 2, let your creative side take over and present in whichever way you deem pretty. You can score, slice and sear the remaining foie gras and serve for a hot/cold contrast, its DELICIOUS.

Photo by Linda Blue

SAVOIR FAIRE CATERING
Sweet Corn Soup with Dungeness Crab
Recipe Courtesy Chef Karen Warner-Smith

Servings: 4
Prep Time: I hour 20 minutes

Ingredients for the Sweet Corn Soup with Dungeness Crab:
4-6 ears of fresh corn, shucked and silk removed
4 tablespoons butter
I cup Yukon Gold Potatoes, peeled and diced
I 1/2 cups yellow onion, diced
I tablespoon fresh thyme leaves
1/4 cup cilantro
Kosher salt
8 cups of corn stock or water
freshly ground pepper
8 ounces of fresh Dungeness crab
I Serrano chile, seeded, finely diced
4 tablespoons olive oil
2 tablespoons crème fraîche

SAVOIR FAIRE CATERING

901 Philinda Avenue
Santa Barbara, CA 93103
www.savoirfairesb.com

805.963.9397

Directions for the Sweet Corn Stock:
With a sharp kitchen knife, cut the tip off each ear of corn for stability. Rest each ear on the cut side, then cut the corn kernels from the cob. Set the kernels aside. Place the cobs in large stockpot and cover with 8 cups water. Bring to a boil, then reduce the heat and simmer for at least twenty minutes or until the broth has taken on a sweet, corn flavor. Strain the stock. Leftovers can be frozen for future recipes.

Directions for the Sweet Corn Soup with Dungeness Crab:
Melt the butter in a large saucepan over medium heat until the butter starts to foam. Add the potato, onion, and thyme. Reduce the heat to low and cook about 10 minutes until the onion is soft and the potatoes appear creamy.

Turn the heat up to high and stir in the corn, cilantro, and I 1/2 teaspoons salt. Stir until it is coated with the butter. Add the stock or water and bring to a boil. Turn the heat down to low and simmer for about 30 minutes, stirring occasionally until the corn and potatoes are tender but not mushy.

Strain the soup over a large bowl or pot. Put half the corn mixture into the blender with a cup of corn stock. Process on low speed to purée the corn. Turn to high speed and blend the soup, adding more stock as needed, until it is completely smooth. Transfer to a clean pot and repeat with remaining corn. For a very smooth consistency, strain the soup through a sieve, pressing through all of the liquid.

Warm the soup and adjust seasoning to taste with salt and pepper. Add more liquid if needed for the desired consistency. You may not need to use all the stock.

Toss together the crab, chile, olive oil and crème fraîche. Season with a little salt and more chile, if desired.

To serve, ladle the warm soup into bowls. Place the crab mixture in the center of each bowl and serve.

Chefs Notes: For a vegetarian version, mix some fresh-diced avocado with a little crème fraîche and fresh lime juice. Ladle the soup over the avocado. This soup is only as good as the sweet corn and crab. Buy the best crab you can and the freshest corn from the summer markets.

SAVOY CAFE' & DELI
Oven-Roasted Beet Salad
Recipe Courtesy Chef Paul Shields

Servings: 2-3
Prep Time: 1 hour

3 large red beets, including beet greens
2 tablespoons extra virgin olive oil, in two parts
sea salt
1 ear fresh corn
1/2 tablespoon maple syrup
1 tablespoon rice wine vinegar

Directions for the Oven-Roasted Beet Salad:
Preheat oven to 350° F .

Peel and dice beets into 1 inch cubes. Toss in a bowl with 1 tablespoon olive oil, then lightly sprinkle with sea salt. Roast in oven for 45-55 minutes, until soft.

While beets are roasting, clean and rough chop the beet greens. Slice corn from the cob and add to the beet greens. In a separate bowl, make vinaigrette by whisking together 1 tablespoon olive oil, maple syrup and rice wine vinegar – set aside.

When the beets are done, place on top of beet greens and corn salad, juices and all. Toss for 20-30 seconds, wilting the greens.

Splash on the vinaigrette, season lightly with sea salt if needed, and enjoy!

SAVOY CAFE' & DELI

24 West Figueroa Street
Santa Barbara, CA 93101
www.thesavoycafe.com

805.962.6611

SAVOY CAFE' & DELI
Turkey Fritters
with Chipotle Mayonnaise
Recipe Courtesy Chef Paul Shields

Servings: 4
PrepTime: 30 minutes

Ingredients for the Turkey Fritters with Chipotle Mayonnaise:
1 tablespoon fresh cilantro leaves
1 teaspoon chipotle in adobe
1 teaspoon salt
zest and juice of 1 lime
1 cup mayonnaise
2 cups cooked turkey meat, shredded
1/4 cup pickled jalapeno, roughly chopped
1 tablespoon pickled jalapeno juice
1 fresh jalapeno, finely minced
1 pasilla chile, julienned
1 russet potato, shredded
1 tablespoon chopped fresh cilantro
1 teaspoon sea salt
1 egg, beaten
2 tablespoons all-purpose flour
1 tablespoon olive oil

Directions for the Chipotle Mayonnaise:
Combine the cilantro, chipotle, salt and lime zest, lime juice and mayonnaise in a food processor and mix for 2 minutes. Let stand for 20 minutes.

Directions for the Turkey Fritters
Preheat the oven to 300° F.

Combine the turkey, pickled jalapeno, pickled jalapeno juice, fresh jalapeno, pasilla, potato, cilantro and salt in a mixing bowl and fold together.

Add the beaten egg and evenly mix into the fritter mixture. Evenly sprinkle the flour on top, then combine to mix in.

Form into 4 patties.

Heat the olive oil in an ovenproof frying pan over medium-high heat and place the fritters in the pan. Cook until golden brown, 3 to 4 minutes, and then flip. Place the frying pan with the fritters in the oven to finish, 4 to 5 minutes.

SAVOY CAFE' & DELI

24 West Figueroa Street
Santa Barbara, CA 93101
www.thesavoycafe.com

805.962.6611

SCARLETT BEGONIA
Charred Cauliflower
with Almond Romesco
Recipe Courtesy Chef Avery Hardin

Servings: 2-4
Prep Time: 45 minutes

Ingredients for the Charred Cauliflower with Almond Romesco:
2 tablespoons Fresno chiles (can be deseeded for less heat)
1/2 cup cider vinegar (Champagne vinegar recommended)
1/4 cup granulated sugar
1/4 cup filtered water
1/2 teaspoon + 2 teaspoons Kosher salt, in two parts
3 sprigs fresh thyme
5 tablespoons extra virgin olive oil, in two parts
3 small shallots, sliced, in two parts
3 cloves garlic, peeled and sliced
2 cups piquillo peppers, roasted
2 teaspoons sherry vinegar (or your favorite vinegar)
2 tablespoons lemon juice, freshly squeezed
1 teaspoon honey
1 1/2 cups almonds, roasted and sliced, plus extra for garnish
1/2 teaspoon red chile flakes (cayenne if you like it spicy)
1/2 teaspoon smoked paprika
2 teaspoons Kosher salt, plus extra to taste
1 teaspoon black pepper, freshly cracked
1 head cauliflower, cut into quarter-sized pieces
(ingredients continued on right)

SCARLETT BEGONIA

11 West Victoria Street, #10
Santa Barbara, CA 93101
www.scarlettbegonia.net

805.770.2143

Ingredients for the Charred Cauliflower (continued):
1/4 cup dry white wine (use quality wine you would drink by itself)
1/4 cup Castelvetrano olives, pitted and sliced, plus extra for garnish
fresh mint for garnish

Directions for the Pickled Fresno Chiles:
Combine all the Fresno chiles, cider vinegar, sugar, 1/4 cup water, 1/2 teaspoon salt and the thyme in a small sauce pot and bring to a boil. Remove from the heat and allow to cool. Add sliced chiles and allow them to pickle for 10-15 minutes.

Directions for the Almond Romesco:
Heat a large sauté pan over medium-high heat with 3 tablespoons of the olive oil. When the pan has reached its smoking point, pull the pan off the heat and add 2 sliced shallots, garlic and peppers. Sauté until the mixture begins to caramelize. Remove from the pan and set aside. Allow to cool slightly. Add to a blender or food processor with the vinegar, lemon juice, honey, almonds, chile flakes, paprika, salt and pepper. Puree the ingredients for three to four minutes or until smooth while slowly adding the oil.

Directions for the Charred Cauliflower:
Place a medium sauté pan over high heat. Add two tablespoons of olive oil and add the cauliflower. Try not to move the cauliflower around too much, as moving it will slow the charring process. Once the cauliflower is charred, add 1 sliced shallot. Continue cooking until slightly translucent. Add the wine and allow it to reduce. Season with salt to taste.

Directions for Assembling the Dish:
Float the mint leaves in cold water to crisp them. Dry and chop the mint. Smear a generous amount of the romesco on a warm plate. Arrange the cauliflower as you please. Garnish with almonds, pickled chile, olives and mint.

Note: The restaurant adds rye crackers baked by Deux Bakery for texture.

CHEF MAYUREE LEELAHATORN - SCHOOL OF CULINARY ARTS & HOTEL MANAGEMENT at SBCC
Gluten-free Canelé

Recipe Courtesy Chef Mayuree Leelahatorn

Servings: 12 two-ounce cakes
Prep Time: 45 minutes

Ingredients for the Gluten-free Canelé:
pan spray for greasing molds
1 1/2 ounces rice flour
1 1/2 ounces almond flour
1/4 teaspoon salt
1 ounce egg yolk
4 1/2 ounces melted butter
1/2 teaspoon vanilla
1/2 teaspoon rum
2 ounces dried apricots, diced
2 ounces pistachio nuts, chopped
4 1/2 ounces egg whites
4 1/2 ounces sugar

Directions for the Gluten-free Canelé:
Preheat the oven to 325° F.

Grease the canelé molds and set on a baking pan. Sift the flours and salt into a medium bowl. Add the egg yolk, butter, vanilla and rum mixing after each addition. Stir in the apricot and the pistachio.

Warm the egg whites and sugar in the top of a double-boiler until the mixture reaches 100°F.

Remove from the double-boiler, then continue to whip until the mixture forms medium peaks. Fold the egg whites into the egg yolk/butter mixture.

Use a 2-ounce scoop and scoop the batter into the canelé molds. Bake for 25 minutes. Cool for 10 minutes then unmold the canelé and serve.

SCHOOL OF CULINARY ARTS at SBCC

721 Cliff Drive
Santa Barbara, CA 93109-2394
www.sbcc.edu/culinaryhotel/index.php

805.965.0581 ext. 2878

Photo by Linda Blue

CHEF RANDY BUBLITZ -
SCHOOL OF CULINARY ARTS & HOTEL
MANAGEMENT at SBCC
Ginger Pear Strudel
Recipe Courtesy Chef Randy Bublitz

Servings: 2-4
Prep Time: 45 minutes

Ingredients for the Ginger Pear Strudel:
 2 pounds pears, peeled and sliced
1/2 cup sugar
2 tablespoons quick-cooking tapioca
 1/2 cup pine nuts
1 tablespoon ginger root, grated
1 teaspoon lemon zest
1 ounce lemon juice
5 sheets phyllo dough (or puff pastry)
1 ounce butter, melted
granulated sugar
crème anglaise

Directions for the Ginger Pear Strudel:
Preheat the oven to 400°F.

Peel, core and THINLY slice the pears. Mix with the sugar, tapioca, nuts, ginger, zest and juice.

Butter each sheet of phyllo. Layer them on top of a clean kitchen towel.

Note: Can substitute puff pastry for phyllo. Use one piece of dough about 10"x15" in size (no need to layer).

Place the pear filling on the phyllo and roll up into a tube using the towel to help roll the pastry. Do not roll too tightly, to allow for expansion.

Brush the top with melted butter and sprinkle with granulated sugar. Bake for 25 minutes.

Serve with crème anglaise.

SCHOOL OF CULINARY ARTS at SBCC

721 Cliff Drive
Santa Barbara, CA 93109-2394
www.sbcc.edu/culinaryhotel/index.php

805.965.0581 ext. 2457

CHEF ROBERTO LOPEZ CARRILLO - SCHOOL OF CULINARY ARTS & HOTEL MANAGEMENT at SBCC
Seafood Enchiladas Rojas

Recipe Courtesy Chef Roberto Lopez Carrillo

Servings: 6
Prep Time: 1 hour 25 minutes

Ingredients for the Seafood Enchiladas Rojas:
6 dried guajillo peppers
3 dried ancho peppers
5 medium tomatoes, in two parts
8 cups chicken broth, in two parts
4 garlic cloves
1 teaspoon Mexican oregano
1/2 teaspoon ground cumin
vegetable oil
salt and pepper
3 medium tomatillos
2 1/2 bunches fresh cilantro, stems removed, in two parts
1/2 red onion, in two parts
2 cups long grain rice
4 ears of corn
2 jalapeno peppers, finely chopped
2 cups cooked black beans
1/4 cup fresh squeezed lemon juice
2 pounds fresh shrimp, bay scallops, local sea bass, calamari squid
12 6" corn tortillas
8 ounces queso fresco
sour cream to garnish

SCHOOL OF CULINARY ARTS at SBCC

721 Cliff Drive
Santa Barbara, CA 93109-2394
www.sbcc.edu/culinaryhotel/index.php

805.965.0581 ext. 2888

Directions for the Red Enchilada Sauce:
Deseed and devein the guajillo and ancho peppers. Cut 3 of the tomatoes into quarters. Put them into a medium-sized pot and boil with 4 cups of chicken broth, the garlic, oregano and cumin until the peppers are soft and tender (about 25 minutes). Set aside until cool enough to handle. Put into a processor and process until smooth. Strain.

In a medium sauce pan over medium-high heat, heat 2 tablespoons of oil, add the pureed tomato mixture, reduce the heat and simmer until thickened. Season to taste with salt and pepper.

Directions for the Cilantro Rice:
Warm 4 cups chicken broth, then put into a food processor with the tomatillos, 2 bunches of cilantro and 1/4 red onion. Puree. In a heavy-bottomed pan with 1/4 cup of oil over medium-high heat, sauté the rice until light brown. Add the broth mixture and 1 1/2 teaspoons salt to the pan. Bring to a soft boil, stir the rice, turn the heat to low, cover and cook until water is absorbed, stirring occasionally. Add warm water and cook longer if needed.

Directions for the Roasted Corn and Black Bean Salsa:
Roast the corn and set aside to cool down before cutting the kernels off the cob. Small dice 2 tomatoes and 1/4 red onion, then add the jalapenos, 1/2 bunch cilantro leaves, black beans and lemon juice. Mix well and season to taste with salt and pepper.

Directions for the Seafood Enchiladas Rojas:
Small dice the seafood. Sauté in 2 teaspoons of oil, then add a small amount of enchilada sauce and keep warm.

In a separate medium sauté pan over medium-high heat, pour enough vegetable oil to soft -fry the tortillas until golden brown but still pliable.

Dip each fried tortilla in the warmed enchilada sauce to coat both sides, then set on a work surface. Place about 2 1/2 ounces of the seafood in the middle of each tortilla with a bit more red sauce, sprinkle queso fresco on top and roll it up. To plate: cover each serving plate with enchilada sauce, add two enchiladas and a scoop of cilantro rice. Cover with more red sauce then spoon the salsa on top and drizzle with sour cream. Enjoy!!!!

Photo by Linda Blue

CHEF SANDRA ALLAIN -
SCHOOL OF CULINARY ARTS & HOTEL
MANAGEMENT at SBCC
Rustic Baguettes

Recipe Courtesy Chef Sandra Allain

Servings: 6 baguettes
Prep Time: 1 hour, plus overnight in the refrigerator

Ingredients for the Rustic Baguettes:
1 pound, 11 ounces bread flour, plus extra for dusting
2 1/4 teaspoons table salt
1 3/4 teaspoons instant yeast or 3 1/2 teaspoons active dry yeast
20 to 24 ounces ice cold water
spray oil to coat the bowl
cornmeal to coat the baking sheet

Directions for the Dough:
Combine the flour, salt and yeast in the bowl of electric mixer fitted with a paddle attachment. Slowly add 20 ounces of the cold water until all the flour is hydrated. Mix on low speed for 2 minutes. Switch to the dough hook and mix for 5 to 6 minutes on medium speed. Add extra water only if the dough is not sticking to the bottom of the bowl. The main part of the dough should be formed into a ball and worked by the dough hook, but the dough has to be soft enough that the bottom of it sticks a bit to the bowl. Mix dough until it becomes smooth, about 10 minutes. Transfer dough to a deep bowl sprayed with oil. Cover top of the bowl with plastic wrap. Refrigerate overnight (or use within three days).

When ready to use, take out the dough and leave at room temperature for 2 to 3 hours.

Directions for the Rustic Baguettes:
Preheat the oven to 475° F.

Transfer the dough to a counter dusted with a liberal amount of flour. Flour the top of the dough and cut into 6 equal portions. Stretch each piece of dough to form a baguette and place on a baking sheet dusted with cornmeal. Dust the loaves with flour and score the top of each with a sharp knife, making parallel diagonal cuts. Place baguettes into the oven and spray with water to create steam. Bake for 20 to 25 minutes until golden brown and the internal temperature is 200° F. Cool before eating.

Note: This dough can also be used to make focaccia and pizza.

SCHOOL OF CULINARY ARTS at SBCC

721 Cliff Drive
Santa Barbara, CA 93109-2394
www.sbcc.edu/culinaryhotel/index.php

805.965.0581 ext. 5173

CHEF STEPHANE RAPP - SCHOOL OF CULINARY ARTS & HOTEL MANAGEMENT at SBCC
Salmon Croissant with Creamy Beurre Blanc Sauce

Recipe Courtesy Chef Stephane Rapp

Servings: 4
Prep Time: 1 hour

Ingredients for the Baby Salmon Croissants:
8 ounces wild salmon fillet
4 4X4-inch puff pastry sheets
extra virgin olive oil
approximately 1 teaspoon fennel seeds, in two parts
approximately 1 teaspoon saffron threads, in two parts
sea salt and freshly ground black pepper
egg wash
2 shallots, sliced finely
approximately 3 tablespoons unsalted butter, in two parts
1/2 cup dry champagne
1 cup heavy cream

Directions for the Baby Salmon Croissants:
Preheat the oven to 350° F.

Slice the salmon into 8 pieces, approximately 2 x1/2 inch strips. Cut each puff pastry square into two equal triangles. Place one salmon strip close to the base of a triangle. Season each with 1 drop of oil, 2 fennel seeds, a saffron thread, sea salt and pepper. Roll each triangle onto itself while curving it slightly to obtain a croissant shape. Use egg wash to moisten the tip of the triangle to seal it to the main part of the dough. Brush each with egg wash. Place on a parchment-lined sheet pan and bake until golden, about 15 minutes.

Directions for the Creamy Beurre Blanc Sauce:
Sweat the shallot in a small amount of butter until translucent. Add 1/2 teaspoon fennel, 1/2 teaspoon saffron and the champagne and bring to a boil. Reduce heat to a simmer and reduce the liquid by half.

Pour in the heavy cream and simmer until the cream has reduced by half. Increase heat to medium-high, and rapidly whisk in 2 tablespoons butter, piece by piece until it has melted into the cream and the sauce is thickened. Strain the sauce through a mesh strainer and adjust seasoning with salt and pepper. Serve immediately.

SCHOOL OF CULINARY ARTS at SBCC

721 Cliff Drive
Santa Barbara, CA 93109-2394
www.sbcc.edu/culinaryhotel/index.php

805.965.0581 ext. 2459

Photo by Linda Blue

CHEF VINCENT VANHECKE - SCHOOL OF CULINARY ARTS & HOTEL MANAGEMENT at SBCC
California Bouillabaise with Rouille

Recipe Courtesy Chef Vincent Vanhecke
Servings: 8
Prep time: 1 hour 30 minutes

Ingredients for the California Boullabaise with Rouille:
1 cup olive oil, in two parts
12 ounces onion, chopped
4 ounces leek chopped
1 1/2 ounces garlic, chopped
4 ounces fennel, sliced
4 ounces long grain rice
8 ounces potatoes, diced 1/4"
750 ml Sauvignon Blanc (1 bottle), in two parts
6 large ripe tomatoes, skinned and finely chopped
4 ounces tomato paste
1/2 ounces orange zest
1 generous pinch good quality saffron
1 bouquet garni (fresh parsley sprigs, fresh thyme, and bay leaf tied
   into a bouquet)
4 pounds fish
1 1/2 pounds shrimp, peeled and deveined
4 ounces chopped shallots
1 1/2 pounds black mussels
(continued on right)

SCHOOL OF CULINARY ARTS

721 Cliff Drive
Santa Barbara, CA 93109-2394
www.sbcc.edu/culinaryhotel/index.php

805.965.0581

Ingredients (continued from left):
1 1/2 pounds clams
1 pound scallops
1/2 teaspoon cayenne
1 pound crab meat
2 ounces Pernod
salt and pepper
1 ounce parsley, chopped
garlic-rubbed crostini

Ingredients for Rouille:
4 cloves garlic
2 small red chiles
4 ounces cooked potatoes
2 ounces olive oil
4-6 ounces fish broth with
   1 pinch saffron added

Directions for the California Boullabaise with Rouille:
Put 3/4 cup of olive oil in a casserole or large sauce pan and sweat (cook without browning) the onion, leek, garlic, fennel, rice and potato until translucent. Add half the wine and reduce the liquid by half. Add the tomato, tomato paste, orange zest, saffron, bouquet garni, the fish, shrimp and sufficient water to cover. Bring to a boil, then turn down the heat to simmer for 15 minutes. Remove the bouquet garni. Remove the seafood (plus some fish if you want--the rest will be blended into the broth) and reserve, keeping warm.

Meanwhile, sweat the shallots in the remaining 1/4 cup olive oil in a separate sauce pan. Add the mussels, clams, and scallops. Add the remaining 375 ml wine, cover the casserole and cook for 7-8 minutes.

Add the broth from the mussel/clams/scallops to the vegetable mixture. Add the cayenne pepper. Blend thoroughly and strain the broth through a china cap into another sauce pan. Return to the heat and stir in the crab meat and Pernod. Add salt and pepper to taste.

Ladle soup in a bowl. Add the reserved mussels, clams, scallops, shrimp and fish. Garnish with chopped parsley, rouille (recipe follows) and garlic-rubbed crostinis.

Directions for the Rouille:
Either in a mortar (or small food processor), pound (or chop) the garlic and chiles. Add the potato and olive oil and slowly incorporate the broth until smooth. Adjust seasoning with salt and pepper if needed.

Photo by Linda Blue

SEAGRASS RESTAURANT

Mi-Cuit Wild King Salmon with Boudin Noir
Recipe Courtesy Chef Robert Perez

Servings: 4
Prep Time: 8 hours, including 6 hours of chilling

Ingredients for the Wild King Salmon:
1 1/2 quarts water
1 1/2 ounces sugar
3 ounces Kosher salt
2 12-ounce wild King salmon fillets, cut in half
extra virgin olive oil

Ingredients for the Parsnip Puree:
8 ounces parsnip, peeled, finely diced
Kosher salt
pinch cayenne pepper
1 cup heavy cream
2 ounces cold butter, cut up

Ingredients for the Grapefruit and the Boudin Noir:
1 ruby grapefruit, segmented
1 tablespoon extra virgin olive oil
1 tablespoon sugar
2 4 ounce boudin noir
1 tablespoon + 1 teaspoon olive oil, in two parts
Maldon salt flakes
white pepper

Ingredients for the Garnish:
2 ounces blanched organic sweet peas, seasoned to taste with
    butter, salt and oregano
lemon juice
salmon roe
micro greens

SEAGRASS RESTAURANT

30 E. Ortega Street
Santa Barbara, CA 93101

www.seagrassrestaurant.com
805.963.1012

Directions for the Salmon:
Heat 3/4 quart water with the sugar and salt long enough to dissolve. Remove from heat, then pour into a bowl and place bowl into a ice water bath. Add remaining water. Once cold, place salmon fillets into a pan large enough to hold the fillets and pour brine over fish to cover. Brine fillets for 45 minutes and remove and pat dry. Place fillets into a lightly oiled zip lock bag, zip closed and place bags into a hot water bath held at 106°F for approximately 50 minutes. (10 minutes after dropping the bags into the water bath, gently agitate the fillets to ensure they are evenly coated with oil and to make it easier to remove them from the bag after cooking.) Using a sous vide machine is the same process and the best way to go. Once cooked, submerge the fish still in the zip lock bag into an ice water bath for 10 to 20 minutes. Once cold, place fillets in the refrigerator for 6 hours in order for the texture to set.

Directions for the Parsnip Puree:
Place parsnip in a stainless steel pot and add cream. Season lightly with Kosher salt and cayenne powder. Cover and gently boil until tender. Pour into a blender, while running the blender, slowly pour in the cream and adjust the thickness with hot water if needed. Add butter and puree until smooth. Strain though a fine mesh strainer and cool. Refrigerate.

Directions for the Grapefruit and the Boudin Noir:
Gently season the segments with 1 tablespoon oil and sugar, place in an ovenproof dish and caramelize in a salamander or under the grill until golden brown.

Oil the boudin noir with 1 teaspoon olive oil. Slice at a 45° angle, creating twelve 1/4" slices (2-3 slices per plate needed). Blanch sweet peas, then warm in butter. Season to taste with salt and nutmeg.

Directions to Finish the Wild King Salmon with Boudin Noir:
Preheat oven to 350°F. Preheat enough olive oil to just cover the salmon fillets to 120°F. Place portions of salmon in the oil for 10 to 15 minutes to warm. Put the sliced and oiled boudin noir into a pan and warm in the oven for approximately 6 minutes and remove pan from oven. Gently remove salmon from oil and place on paper towels. Season with Maldon salt and white pepper.

Spoon a small amount of parsnip puree in the center of the plates with a spoon and run the spoon through the puree to create a ribbon. Lay three slices of boudin noir on each plate, just off center against the parsnip puree. Place a salmon fillet on top of the puree leaning against the sausage. Spoon the sweet peas onto the plate. Squeeze a little lemon juice over the salmon and sprinkle lightly with Maldon salt.

Place decorated plates in the oven for 3 minutes and remove. Top the salmon with a dab of salmon roe and garnish with micro greens.

Photo by Fran Collin

SEASONS CATERING
Green Bean Salad
with Preserved Lemon
Recipe Courtesy Gabrielle Moes

Servings: 10
Prep Time: 1 hour, plus 2 weeks preserving

Ingredients for the Green Bean Salad with Preserved Lemon:
5 lemons
Kosher salt
2 tablespoons + 1 teaspoon salt, in two parts
3 pounds small tender green beans, trimmed
1/2 cup extra virgin olive oil
1 teaspoon Dijon mustard
1 teaspoon salt
black pepper
1/4 cup lemon juice
1/4 bunch mint

Directions for the Preserved Lemon:
Cut an X shape on the top of the lemons and fill with Kosher salt. Be very generous as the lemons need to be drowned with salt to break down the peel. Place in a container big enough to fit all lemons, but small enough to keep lemons tight together. Keep in the refrigerator for 2 weeks. The remainder can be used for up to 2 months.

Directions for the Green Bean Salad:
Add 2 tablespoons salt to a medium pot of water and bring to a boil. Add the green beans and blanch for 3-5 minutes. Drain and chill on ice to stop cooking.

Directions for the Lemon Vinaigrette:
Whisk together the oil, Dijon mustard, 1 teaspoon salt, a pinch of black pepper and the lemon juice.

Wash and pluck the mint leaves and set aside.

Cut half the preserved lemons into wedges and cut out the pith (the white inner skin of lemon peel) so only the yellow skin is remaining. Small dice the yellow peel.

Dress the green beans with half the vinaigrette, half the preserved lemon, half the mint and a good sprinkle of salt. Adjust seasonings to taste, adding more dressing or salt if needed. Bowl up and garnish with the rest of the preserved lemon and mint.

SEASONS CATERING

2646 Palma Drive #255
Ventura, CA 93003
www.seasonscateringca.com

805.339.9665
Santa Barbara Culinary Arts | page 134

Photo by Linda Blue

THE SHALHOOB FUNK ZONE PATIO CUTTING ROOM

Grilled Boneless Half-Chicken "Sandwich" Stuffed with Garlic-Braised Spinach, Oven-Cured Local Tomato, Feta and Basil

Recipe Courtesy Chef Pete Clements

Servings: 2
Prep Time: 3 hours 30 minutes

Ingredients for the Grilled Half-Chicken Sandwich, Garlic-Braised Spinach and Oven-Cured Tomato:
4 local tomatoes, quartered with seeds removed
extra virgin olive oil
1 teaspoon dried thyme leaves
Kosher salt
freshly ground black pepper
2 pounds fresh spinach
2 cloves garlic, minced
1 chicken completely de-boned, portioned into two halves, skin intact (butcher will do this for you)
8 large basil leaves, stem removed
6 ounces fresh feta cheese, crumbled

THE SHALHOOB FUNK ZONE PATIO CUTTING ROOM

220 Gray Avenue
Santa Barbara, CA 93101
www.funkzonepatio.com

805.963.7733

Directions for Oven-Cured Tomato:
Preheat the oven to 200° F.

Toss the quartered and seeded tomatoes in 4 tablespoons of extra virgin olive oil, the thyme, 1 teaspoon of Kosher salt and 1/2 teaspoon of freshly ground black pepper. Place on a baking sheet lined with foil or parchment and bake for 3 hours, then remove.

Directions for Braised Spinach and Garlic:
Cook fresh spinach and minced garlic in 3 tablespoons of extra virgin olive oil for 5 minutes on medium high heat, then drain.

Directions for the Grilled Boneless Half Chicken Sandwich:
Preheat barbeque, char grill or gas grill to medium high heat. Turn up the oven to 425° F.

Lay out the chicken halves on a work surface, season with Kosher salt and fresh pepper on both sides. Lightly drizzle extra virgin olive oil on both sides.

Grill chicken halves for 4 to 5 minutes on each side, making sure to get some good grill marks on the skin side and some light color on the meat side. Remove from heat and let rest for 6 to 8 minutes.

Lay the grilled pieces of chicken out flat on a clean work surface, season with Kosher salt and fresh pepper and drizzle with extra virgin olive oil. Lay basil leaves down flat on each piece, then place equal portions of braised spinach on each of the pieces followed by the oven-cured tomato and the crumbled feta.

Fold one side over to make a "sandwich". Repeat with the other piece. Place on a foil or parchment-lined baking sheet, then roast for 18 minutes or until the inside temperature is 160° F.

Remove from oven, let rest for 6 minutes, then serve with an arugula salad!

SIDES HARDWARE & SHOES -
a BROTHERS RESTAURANT
Roasted Beet and Goat Cheese Salad
Recipe Courtesy Chef Michael Cherney

Servings: 4
Prep Time: 2 hours

Ingredients for the Roasted Beet and Goat Cheese Salad:
4 3/4 cups sherry vinegar, in two parts
1 cup sugar
14 red baby beets
1/4 cup olive oil
1 head of garlic, peeled
1 bunch fresh thyme
1 1/2 tablespoon Dijon mustard
1 tablespoon clover honey
4 cups grapeseed oil
salt and pepper
1/2 cup goat cheese
1/2 cup toasted and crushed walnuts
2 Belgian endive
20 leaves micro red sorrel

Directions for the Roasted Beet and Goat Cheese Salad:
Preheat the oven to 350° F. Make a sherry gastrique by whisking together and reducing 4 cups of the sherry vinegar with the sugar over low heat until the consistency of syrup. To check, spread a spoonful on a cool plate. If the reduction sticks to the plate and runs down slowly, it is done. Let cool to room temperature and place in a squeeze bottle. (continued at right)

SIDES HARDWARE & SHOES

2375 Alamo Pintado Avenue
Los Olivos CA 93441
www.sidesrestaurant.com
sidesrestaurant@gmail.com
805.688.4820

Directions (continued from left):
Wash the beets under cold running water to remove all the dirt. Cut off the greens and save for another dish--they are very tasty!). Reserve 4 of the beets for shaving raw later.

Toss the remaining 10 beets in olive oil, salt, pepper, garlic cloves and thyme. Put an inch of cold water inside a baking dish and cover with a sheet of aluminum foil. Place the tossed beets inside the foil. The water prevents the beets from getting burnt or scalded by the bottom of the roasting pan. Cover the top with foil. Make sure all the edges are sealed so no water escapes. Roast for 1 hour or until tender. Check doneness with a tooth pick.

When the beets are ready, take the aluminum and plastic off and let the beets cool until you can touch them with your hands. Use a towel and rub off the skin, then cut each beet into quarters. Place into the refrigerator until ready to serve.

Take the 4 clean beets you have set aside. Prepare an ice bath. Using a mandoline, shave the beets very thin into the ice bath. Let the shaved beets stay in the ice bath for a few minutes until they slightly curl and get nice and crunchy. Drain onto a paper towel and set aside.

Combine the remaining 3/4 cup sherry vinegar, the Dijon mustard, and honey. Whisk together. Slowly drizzle in 4 cups grapeseed oil. Season with salt and pepper. Note: you will have extra dressing for future use.

Put the goat cheese in a piping bag and pipe into a single straight line onto a parchment lined baking sheet. Using a paring knife, make a cut every inch. Gently pick up the goat cheese, one at a time and roll in crushed walnuts. Do not stack finished goat cheese on top of one another. Keep chilled until ready to serve.

Directions for Assembling the Dish:
Cut each endive into quarters and toss with sherry vinaigrette, salt and pepper. In a different bowl, toss the roasted beets with the raw shaved beets, sherry vinaigrette, salt and pepper. Garnish the plate with sherry gastrique on the bottom, and arrange endive, raw beets and roasted beets as desired. Add a few pieces of walnut crusted goat cheese and garnish with red sorrel. Serve and enjoy!

SLY'S
Chocolate Soufflé
Recipe Courtesy Chef James Sly

Servings: 4 8-ounce soufflés
Prep Time: 45 minutes

Ingredients for the Chocolate Souffle:
3/4 cup milk, whole
1/2 vanilla bean
2 each egg yolks, fresh
granulated sugar
salt
4 teaspoons all-purpose flour
7 ounces dark chocolate, 76%, chopped
powdered sugar, for dusting
butter, room temperature for greasing soufflé cups
6 ounces fresh egg whites
1 teaspoon lemon juice

Note: Everybody loves chocolate! Nothing beats the sweet smell of a chocolate soufflé, heading through a dining room to your table. We do chocolate soufflés at Sly's for special occasions, as a special end to a special dinner. Much has been said about the difficulty of making a soufflé, most of it an exaggeration. Soufflés are simple, fun and delicious. A chocolate soufflé is even easier to make than most other flavors - the rich chocolate helps hold the soufflé together as it rises.

SLY'S

686 Linden Avenue
Carpinteria, CA 93103
www.slysonline.com

805.684.6666

Directions for the Pastry Cream:
Scald the milk with the vanilla bean in a non-reactive pan like stainless steel. Do not burn the bottom! While the milk is heating, beat the egg yolks with 3 1/2 tablespoons sugar and a pinch of salt. Stop when they reach the ribbon stage. (The yolk-sugar mixture flows in a thick ribbon from the end of the whisk). Add the flour and stir just enough to mix in thoroughly. Do not over beat.

Temper the mixture by pouring a bit of the hot milk into the yolk mixture, whisking constantly. Add the remaining hot milk while stirring. Return to the pan, and stir constantly over low heat until the pastry cream comes to a boil. Cook for 20 seconds or so. Remove from the heat and immediately pour into a bowl to cool. Stir in the chopped chocolate so that it can melt into the pastry cream. Mix well, then dust with powdered sugar to prevent a skin from forming.

Directions for the Souffl:é
Preheat the oven to 425° F.

Butter the interiors and outer rims of four 8-ounce soufflé dishes. Fill a soufflé dish about half way with granulated sugar, then tilt the mold while rotating to let any excess sugar fall into the next mold. Continue until all 4 are done.

Using an electric mixer, add the egg whites, lemon juice and a pinch of salt to a clean, grease-free bowl. Beat the egg whites to soft peaks, then gradually beat in 4 tablespoons of sugar. Continue to beat until the whites are stiff but not dry; do not overbeat. Fold a large spoonful of the beaten whites into the soufflé base, mixing in, then fold the base into the remaining whites just until blended.

Divide the mixture among the prepared dishes, filling to about 1/4 inch from the top. An ice cream scoop works well for this. Run a knife around the inside edge of each dish to about halfway down to release the batter from the side of the dish.

Place the dishes in a small baking pan, and add enough hot water to the pan to come about 1/4 inch up the side of the dishes. Bake until the soufflés are well-risen and lightly browned, about 13 minutes. Dust the top with powdered sugar, and serve immediately to your very impressed friends.

SLY'S
Spaghettini with Calamari in a Spicy Red Sauce
Recipe Courtesy Chef James Sly

Servings: 4 generous servings
Prep Time: 15 minutes

Ingredients for the Spaghettini with Calamari:
1 pound small calamari, cleaned and sliced into 1/4 " rings
salt and freshly ground black pepper
2 teaspoons or more red chile, crushed
1 pound dry spaghettini (thin spaghetti)
2 ounces olive oil
24 ounces marinara (red sauce)
2 tablespoons Italian parsley, coarsely chopped

Note: Since the Italians traditionally do not serve grated cheese with fish, cheese is not included in this recipe.

SLY'S

686 Linden Avenue
Carpinteria, CA 93103
www.slysonline.com

805.684.6666

Directions for the Spaghettini with Calamari:
Smaller squid are best and including tentacles in the dish even better. Sprinkle the squid with salt, freshly ground black pepper and crushed red chile. Use as much as you like-2 teaspoons will make the dish just moderately spicy.

Get everything ready to prepare the dish: warm the sauce, have the chopped parsley on hand, select the sauté pan for the calamari and sauce, a colander for draining the pasta and warm serving plates. Cook the pasta: bring 4 quarts of water to a boil and add 2 1/2 ounces of salt before adding the pasta. The Italian rule for salt is "10, 100, 1000": 10 grams of salt for 100 grams of pasta in 1 liter of water.) The amount of salt is important, it will make your pasta taste better.

Cook the pasta until al dente - slightly resistant to the bite - then drain. Reserve 2-3 ounces of the pasta water. Put the drained spaghettini back in the warm pot with the reserved pasta cooking water. Heat the olive oil over high heat in a shallow, thick bottomed sauté pan until hot. Carefully put in the calamari, stirring as it cooks for no more than 30 seconds. The oil will sputter, so be careful. Carefully add the warm marinara sauce, then toss in the pasta and the 2-3 ounces of the reserved pasta water.

Arrange in the warm plates and top with the coarsely chopped Italian parsley.

Note: This is a fast, simple and delicious pasta to make and a popular one at Sly's. If you have the marinara sauce already made (or if you "cheat" and buy a jar of marinara sauce) the whole process can take as little as 15 minutes, most of which is waiting for the water to boil. Naturally, you can make it as spicy or as mild as you'd like - and if, like one of our regular customers at Sly's, you prefer linguini to spaghettini, the process is exactly the same.

Buon Appetito! from Sly's.

Photo by Linda Blue

TAMA TAKAHASHI, FOOD EDITOR
Steak Teriyaki
Recipe Courtesy Tama Takahashi

Servings: 4
Prep Time: 15 minutes

Ingredients for the Steak Teriyaki:
4 sirloin steaks or filet mignon, trimmed of fat
salt
1 tablespoon safflower oil
1 tablespoon sesame oil (for flavor)
4 tablespoons sake (Japanese rice wine)
3 tablespoons mirin (Japanese cooking wine)
2 tablespoons dark soy sauce (koikuchi)
1 teaspoon fresh ginger, minced
1 tablespoon garlic, minced
1 tablespoon brown sugar

Directions for the Steak Teriyaki:
Lightly salt the meat on both sides. Let sit 2 minutes, then pat dry with paper towels. Have all your ingredients measured and ready.

In the meantime, turn on the hood fan to high as the browning process will produce a quantity of smoke. Heat the oil in a sauté pan over high heat. Sear the steaks on one side for 3 minutes. Turn the steaks and drizzle with the sake. Sear for another 3 minutes.

The steaks should be well-browned but rare inside. Set aside.

Add the mirin, soy sauce, ginger, garlic and brown sugar to the pan and boil until the sauce is reduced to a glaze that will coat the back of a spoon.

Return the steaks to the pan and cook for a minute, turning to coat with sauce. Remove to a cutting board, let sit for 3 minutes, then slice and plate. Drizzle some of the sauce on top.

Note: Many people have never had true teriyaki because it is a reduction glaze, not a sauce that comes out of a jar! I add ginger, garlic and brown sugar to make the flavor more robust so it can pair with a Santa Barbara Syrah.

TAMA TAKAHASHI
santabarbaraculinaryarts@yahoo.com

805.302.0565

TOMA RESTAURANT & BAR
Channel Islands White Sea Bass with Braised Fennel, Petite Potato, Cracked Green Olive Brown Butter and Herb Salad

Recipe Courtesy Chef Nat Ely

Servings: 4
Prep Time: 2 hours, 15 minutes

Ingredients for the Seabass with Braised Fennel:
2 medium fennel bulbs, tops removed, split in half
1/2 cup white wine
3 tablespoons + 1/4 pound butter, in two parts
salt
1 bay leaf
1 quart vegetable or chicken stock
1 pound mixed petite or fingerling potatoes
olive oil
pepper
1/2 cup Castelvetrano olives, pitted and broken
1/4 bunch parsley leaves
1/4 bunch cilantro
1/4 bunch purple basil
1/4 bunch dill fronds
4 pieces of local seabass fillets, skin removed
1 teaspoon olive oil

Directions for the Seabass with Braised Fennel:
Preheat oven to 350° F.

Place the fennel in a small pot or braising pan with the wine, 3 tablespoons butter, 1 teaspoon salt, bay leaf and stock. Cover with lid and place in the oven to bake for 2 hours or until the fennel is tender yet firm. Let cool in the liquid. Split the fennel halves into 3 pieces per half. Reserve the braising liquid.

The potatoes can be kept whole or split, depending on their size. Lightly coat them with olive oil, season with salt and pepper, then roast in the oven on a sheet pan for about 35 minutes or until tender.

Place 1/4 pound butter into a saucepan and heat over medium-high heat, whisking until it turns a light to medium brown. Pour into a cool container, preferably heavy duty glass or steel. After the butter has cooled, add the olives. Remove the stems of the parsley, cilantro, basil and dill. Toss the leaves together in a small bowl.

Pat the fillets dry, then lightly season with salt and pepper. Pan fry the seabass in the oil in a medium hot pan. Cook about 4 minutes on each side.

Directions for Assembling the Dish:
In individual serving bowls, place warm potatoes and fennel. Next spoon on top two ounces of warm fennel-braising liquid. Add the pan-roasted sea bass fillet, top with a large spoonful of the cracked-olive butter and finish with a nice pinch of the fresh herbs.

TOMA RESTAURANT & BAR

324 West Cabrillo Boulevard
Santa Barbara, CA 93101
www.tomarestaurant.com

805.962.0777

TOURING & TASTING Magazine
Filet Mignon Steak Bites with Arugula and Horseradish Cream

Recipe Courtesy Food Editor Tama Takahashi

Servings: 4
Prep Time: 30 minutes

Ingredients for the Filet Mignon Steak Bites with Arugula and Horseradish Cream:

2 large Yukon gold or other waxy potatoes
2 filet mignon
salt
approximately 2 tablespoons safflower oil
1 tablespoon garlic, finely minced
1 tablespoon fresh tarragon, finely minced or 1/2 tablespoon dry
2 teaspoons soy sauce
1 tablespoon Worcestershire sauce
1 tablespoon sugar
a few turns of freshly ground black pepper
3 tablespoons Westerly Cabernet Sauvignon
3 tablespoons sour cream
1 teaspoon finely grated or finely minced onion
1/2 teaspoon lemon juice
1/8 teaspoon white pepper
approximately 1 1/2 teaspoons horseradish
arugula for garnish
approximately 1 tablespoon chopped chives, for garnish

TOURING & TASTING Magazine

35 South La Patera Lane, Suite C.
Goleta, CA 93117
www.touringandtasting.com

800.850.4370

Directions for the Filet Mignon Steak Bites with Arugula and Horseradish Cream:

Put the potatoes in a small pot and fill with water to cover. Bring to a boil and cook until they can easily be pierced with a fork. Plunge into an ice bath to cool, then drain. Slice 1/4" thick, on a slight diagonal, and remove peel. (Do not use baking or Idaho potatoes as these will fall apart in the appetizer.)

Trim the filet mignon so the sides are even. Keep the trimmings for another use (for example, cook in the leftover glaze from this recipe). Sprinkle them lightly with salt and put on a paper towel.

Have all your ingredients pre-measured. Put the garlic, tarragon, soy sauce, Worcestershire sauce, brown sugar and pepper into a small bowl and stir to combine. Adjust seasonings to taste. Measure the Westerly Cabernet Sauvignon into another small bowl.

Skim the bottom of a cast-iron or sauté pan with a thin layer of oil. Heat until very hot but do not let the oil smoke or burn. Pat the filet mignon dry with paper towels, then sear them on all sides. They should sizzle as they cook. Turn every 20 seconds or so to brown nicely on all sides and to cook the outer 1/4 of meat. Remove to a side plate. Pour the Westerly Cabernet into the hot pan. Stir with a wooden spoon, scraping up any meat bits left in the pan. Add the soy sauce mixture and continue stirring. The sauce should bubble and reduce quickly. When it has thickened, put the steaks back in and turn several times to coat each side a few times with the reduced sauce. Take the pan off the heat, remove the steaks to a side plate and let rest for 10 minutes before slicing.

Mix the sour cream, onion, lemon juice and white pepper together in a small bowl. Adjust seasonings to taste with salt and horseradish. Spread a thin layer of horseradish cream on each potato oval. Sprinkle with arugula, then top with the filet mignon slices and chopped chives .

Created to pair with the Westerly 2010 Cabernet Sauvignon.

Photo by Tama Takahashi

TRATTORIA ULIVETO
Ravioli di Spinaci, Burro e Salvia
Recipe Courtesy Chef Alfonso Curti

Servings: 8-10
Prep time: 1 hour 30 minutes, plus overnight pickling

Ingredients for the Ravioli di Spinaci, Burro e Salvia:
2 eggs
2 1/2 cups ricotta cheese
1/4 teaspoon grated nutmeg
pinch of salt
8 ounces Parmesan cheese, grated, plus extra for topping
6 ounces bread crumbs
15 ounces fresh spinach, blanched
fresh pasta dough
semolina flour for dusting work surface
1 stick butter
1 clove garlic, finely chopped
1 bunch fresh sage leaves

Directions for the Ravioli di Spinaci, Burro e Salvia:
Lightly beat the eggs in a large bowl. Add the ricotta, nutmeg, pinch of salt, 8 ounces Parmesan and bread crumbs, then mix well. Fold in the blanched and drained spinach.

Roll out the fresh pasta dough thinly. in batches. (Keep the rest of the dough covered with plastic wrap or a damp kitchen towel.) Cut two long rectangular strips of dough of about 3 inches across. Dot a generous amount of filling every 3 inches along one piece of the dough. Place the other sheet on top and press it lightly all along the edges. Trim the edges of each ravioli with a pastry wheel. Seal the edges by pressing the two layers together all around the edges. Lay them on a tray with some semolina flour on the bottom to avoid sticking.

Boil a large pot of water with a handful of Kosher salt. Cook the ravioli until they are just "al dente", then drain.

While the water is heating, melt the butter in a saucepan over medium-low and sweat the garlic. Add the sage leaves and cook briefly.

Dress the ravioli with the sage butter and sprinkle with Parmesan cheese.

Buon appetito!

TRATTORIA ULIVETO

285 Broadway Street
Orcutt, CA 93455
www.trattoriauliveto.com

805.934.4546

TRE LUNE
Calamari alla Griglia
Recipe Courtesy Chef Cesar Lara

Servings: 1
Prep Time: 30 minutes

Ingredients for Calamari Alla Griglia:
8 ounces calamari
3 tablespoons extra virgin olive oil, in two parts
3 garlic cloves, minced, in two parts
2 teaspoons bread crumbs
2 teaspoons fresh parsley, chopped, in two parts
salt and pepper
4 ounces fresh spinach, steamed
2 celery stalks, sliced
2 small red rose potatoes, boiled and thinly sliced
2 tablespoons vine ripened tomato, chopped
lemon slices for garnish

Directions for the Calamari Alla Griglia:
Preheat oven to 350° F. Heat a grill.

Clean the calamari with cold water. Fill an 8-quart pan with water and bring to a boil. Add the calamari then remove from heat, allowing calamari to sit for 15 minutes. Begin preparing all the other ingredients while calamari are cooking, then remove calamari and cool before slicing into rings.

Using a large sauté pan over medium heat, add 1 tablespoon olive oil and 1 clove minced garlic, sauté for one minute. Combine with the calamari, bread crumbs, 1 teaspoon parsley and a pinch of salt and pepper. Sauté for 5 minutes, then place in the oven for another 5 minutes.

In a separate sauce pan over medium heat, add the 2 tablespoons olive oil and sauté the remaining garlic and the spinach. Season to taste with salt and pepper.

Remove the calamari from the oven and continue cooking over medium heat on grill. Fold in the celery and potato, sautéing for 3 minutes. Place cooked spinach on center of plate, place calamari on bed of spinach and finish with tomato and parsley.

Garnish with lemon.

TRE LUNE

1151 Coast Village Road
Montecito, CA 93108
www.trelunesb.com

805.969.2646

VALLE VERDE
Peaches Penelope
Recipe Courtesy Executive Chef Jake Reimer

Servings: 4
Prep Time: 45 minutes plus 6+ hours chill time

Ingredients for the Peaches Penelope:
1/4 cup peach puree
1/2 cup granulated sugar
1/2 cup flour
1 quart + 2 cups simple syrup, in two parts
4 sprigs fresh lavender
4 leaves fresh lemon verbena
4 ounces late harvest wine (Sauternes, etc.)
seeds of 1 fresh vanilla bean
1 pound white or yellow peaches + 2 white peaches, in two parts
1 teaspoon grenadine
1 tablespoon powdered candied ginger
1 tablespoon lime juice
1 tablespoon apple juice
1/4 cup agar agar
2 1/4 cups raspberry puree
1/2 cup confectionary sugar
1 teaspoon lime zest, finely minced
2 cups whipped heavy cream

Directions for the Peaches Penelope:
Preheat oven to 325° F.

Whisk together the peach puree, granulated sugar and flour. Cool, preferably overnight. Spread a thin layer on parchment covered cookie sheet or silpat. Bake for about 5-6 minutes until just starting to color. Remove from oven and transfer to chilled surface. Break cookie to desired shape.

Combine 1 quart simple syrup, lavender, verbena, Sauternes and vanilla bean in a sauce pot. Peel and core 1 pound peaches and add to syrup mix along with the grenadine. Bring to light simmer and cook lightly covered for about 6 minutes or until peaches are just softening. Cool down to 40° F in the liquid, 6 hours or overnight.

Puree white peaches with 2 cups simple syrup and ginger. Add lime and apple juices and bring to a simmer. Whisk in agar agar until thickened (so it coats a spoon). Pour onto a cookie sheet or sheet pan until cool. Bring to 40° F before serving.

Combine the raspberry puree, confectionary sugar, zest and whipped cream in a chilled bowl and fold lightly together. Bring down to 40° F before serving.

Note: This recipe From our Chef's Wine Dinners. A new take on a French classic.

VALLE VERDE

900 Calle De Los Amigos
Santa Barbara, CA 93105
www.Valleverde.org

805.883.4000

Valle Verde Retirement Community is owned and operated by ABHOW. SODEXO is partners with ABHOW to bring the very best in today's dining scene as showcased by Executive Chef Jake Reimer, Chef de Cuisine Kevin Abernathy and Executive Sous Chef Herve Blondin.

VIA MAESTRA 42
Pollo alla Valdostana
Recipe Courtesy Proprietor Renato Moiso

Servings: 4
Prep Time: 40 minutes

Ingredients for the Pollo alla Valdostana:
4 free-range chicken breasts
1/2 cup "00" flour
2 farm fresh eggs, beaten
1 cup ciabatta breadcrumbs
4 slices Prosciutto Cotto
4 thin slices Prosciutto di Parma
4 slices Fontina Val d'Aosta cheese
6 tablespoons extra virgin olive oil, in two parts
1/4 cup plus 2 tablespoons butter, cubed, in two parts
4 sage leaves, chopped
2 large potatoes
1 tablespoon black truffle sauce
2 tablespoons Grana Padano cheese
2 tablespoons whole milk
2 cups broccoli florets
2 carrots, sliced
2 cloves garlic, sliced
pinch of salt
pinch of white pepper

VIA MAESTRA 42

3343 State Street
Santa Barbara, CA 93105
http://viamaestra42.com

805.569.6522

Directions for the Pollo alla Valdostana:
Preheat the oven to 350° F. Line a baking sheet with aluminum foil; set aside.

Split the side of each chicken breast to form a pocket, making sure not to cut through the other side. Set aside three bowls large enough for the chicken pieces and fill them with the flour, egg and breadcrumbs. Roll one slice each of the Fontina, Prosciutto di Parma and Prosciutto Cotto together. Place a roll inside each chicken pocket, then close the pockets.

Pour 4 tablespoons olive oil into a large pan over medium heat. Dip each chicken breast in flour, egg, and breadcrumbs, respectively, coating both sides. Place battered chicken breasts in the pan with the olive oil, browning each side for approximately 2 minutes. Using tongs, place chicken breasts on a baking sheet and bake for approximately 10 minutes.

While the chicken is baking, heat 1/4 cup butter and sage in a pan for approximately 2 minutes or until lightly browned. Once chicken is finished baking, drizzle browned butter and sage over the chicken.

Mamma, che buono!

Directions for Truffle Mashed Potatoes:
Put a pot of water on to boil. Peel and cube the potatoes. Once water is at a steady boil, add potatoes and boil for approximately 5 minutes. Place potatoes, 2 tablespoons butter, black truffle sauce and milk in a large bowl and mash them together using a large whisk until smooth.

Directions for Mixed Vegetables:
Put water on to boil over high heat; immerse broccoli and carrots for approximately 2 minutes. Gently cook garlic in 2 tablespoons extra virgin olive oil in a pan over medium heat, until golden.

Drain the vegetables and place in the pan with olive oil and garlic; cook for approximately 2 minutes. Season to taste with a pinch of salt and white pepper.

Buon appetito!

Photo by Linda Blue

VIA MAESTRA 42
About Proprietor Renato Moiso

Renato Moiso was born in Cocconato d'Asti, in the Northern Italian region of Piemonte.

Having grown up in the area known for white truffles and Barolo wines, along with hazelnuts and fabulous mountain cheeses, he is well versed in the flavors of Italy. From an early age working in restaurants throughout Italy, Germany and England, he has developed a wonderful sense of hospitality. Nowhere more evident than in Via Maestra 42, the restaurant he and his wife, Lisa, opened in December 2000 in Santa Barbara, California.

In Via Maestra 42, you can find an atmosphere encompassing the best of Italian flavors. Whether you choose to sample some of the delectable cheeses and meats, like the sharp Provolone or the 20-months-aged Prosciutto di Parma, or decide to indulge in the Italian gelato, you will find yourself being carried back to Italy each time you visit.

The vast assortment of regional Italian extra virgin olive oils will allow you to take a taste of Italy home with you.

The menu focuses on traditional, regional dishes, such as Branzino al Forno, Penne al Ragu', Risotto con Funghi Porcini or Brasato al Barbera. These can be paired with their wide selection of Barolo and Brunello di Montalcino among other carefully selected Italian wines.

Renato and his staff look forward to transporting you back to Italy on your next visit to Santa Barbara.

VIA MAESTRA 42

3343 State Street
Santa Barbara, CA 93105
http://viamaestra42.com

805.569.6522

Photo by Linda Blue

WESTERLY
Peach and Goat Cheese Salad
with Kale Microgreens
Recipe Courtesy Food Editor Tama Takahashi

Servings: 4
Prep Time: 1 hour 30 minutes, plus overnight pickling

Ingredients for the Peach and Goat Cheese Salad:
2 large ripe peaches
2 ounces top-quality goat cheese
1 package kale microgreens
1/4 cup extra virgin olive oil
3 tablespoons apple cider vinegar
1 tablespoon finely minced shallot
1/4 teaspon orange zest
1/2 teaspoon salt
freshly ground black pepper

Directions for the Peach and Goat Cheese Salad:
Slice the peaches and plate in a zig zag pattern on narrow serving dishes. Dot the goat cheese among the slices. Top with the microgreens.

Mix the oil, vinegar, shallot, zest, salt and three or four grinds of fresh black pepper in a small bowl. Drizzle over the salad.

Created to pair with the 2013 Westerly Sauvignon Blanc.

92 Points - Wine Enthusiast:

"The nose on this wine, which is now being made by former Harlan Estate cellar master Adam Henkel, is fresh and boisterous with lime sorbet and lemon glacé aromas. The palate is clean and crisp yet quite tropical, with sweetgrass, mango and papaya flavors."
— M.K., Wine Enthusiast (6/1/2015)

WESTERLY
1733 Fletcher Way
Santa Ynez, CA 93460
www,westerlywines.com
info@westerlywines.com
805.693.9300

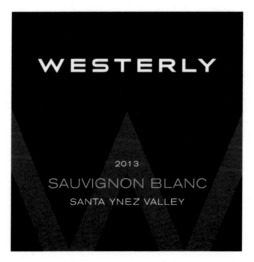

2013
SAUVIGNON BLANC
SANTA YNEZ VALLEY

WINE CASK RESTAURANT
Bouillabaisse with Local Sea Bass
Recipe Courtesy Executive Chef David Rosner

Servings: 4
Prep Time: 3 hours 15 minutes

Ingredients for Bouillabaisse with Local Sea Bass:
3 fennel bulbs
6 red peppers
4 red onions
4 carrots
6 ounces garlic
2 ounces saffron
1/4 bunch basil, stems removed
12 Roma tomatoes
1 pound fish bones from the sea bass for sauce
1 pound baby zucchini
1 pound baby patty pan squash
1 pound baby eggplant
8 ounces piquillo peppers
6 ounces garlic, roasted
4 6-ounce fillets taken from 2.5 pound whole local sea bass
salt and pepper

Directions for the Bouillabaisse Sauce:
Roughly chop the fennel, peppers, onions, carrots, garlic and tomatoes. In a heavy-bottomed stock pot on medium high heat, sweat the vegetables and the saffron and basil until tender with the pot uncovered.

Add the bones and enough water to cover them. Cover the pot and bring to a boil, then turn down to a simmer for 3 hours. Remove bones and blend in a food processor until smooth. Strain through a Chinois or cheesecloth-lined sieve.

Directions for the Vegetables:
In a heavy-bottomed sauté pan, separately sauté the zucchini, patty pan squash, eggplant and Piquillo peppers, then cool them quickly. Reheat before serving with the roasted garlic.

Directions for the Fish:
Preheat the oven to 350°F .

Season fillets with salt and pepper. In a heavy-bottomed sauté pan, brown all sides of the fish in a small amount of oil. Bake for approximately 6 minutes.

Plate the sauce in 4 bowls, arrange the vegetables and fish and serve immediately.

WINE CASK RESTAURANT

813 Anacapa Street
Santa Barbara, CA 93101
www.winecask.com

805.966.9463

Photo by Linda Blue

Photo by Linda Blue